Modern Etudes and Studies
for the Total Percussionist

Modern Etudes and Studies

FOR THE TOTAL PERCUSSIONIST

Second Edition

Chris Colaneri

OXFORD
UNIVERSITY PRESS

OXFORD
UNIVERSITY PRESS

Oxford University Press is a department of the University of Oxford.
It furthers the University's objective of excellence in research, scholarship,
and education by publishing worldwide.

Oxford   New York
Auckland   Cape Town   Dar es Salaam   Hong Kong   Karachi
Kuala Lumpur   Madrid   Melbourne   Mexico City   Nairobi
New Delhi   Shanghai   Taipei   Toronto

With offices in
Argentina   Austria   Brazil   Chile   Czech Republic   France   Greece
Guatemala   Hungary   Italy   Japan   Poland   Portugal   Singapore
South Korea   Switzerland   Thailand   Turkey   Ukraine   Vietnam

Oxford is a registered trade mark of Oxford University Press in the UK and
certain other countries.

Published in the United States of America by
Oxford University Press
198 Madison Avenue, New York, NY 10016

Library of Congress Cataloging-in-Publication Data
Colaneri, Chris.
Modern etudes and studies for the total percussionist / Chris Colaneri. — Second edition.
    pages cm
Includes bibliographical references and index.
ISBN 978-0-19-938914-8 (alk. paper)
1. Percussion instruments—Instruction and study. I. Title.
MT655.C63 2015
372.87'3—dc23
                        2014033332

9 8 7 6 5 4 3 2 1
Printed in the United States of America on acid-free paper

Contents

Contents

Foreword

"If you think about it, drums are the new violins!" So wrote *New York Times* music critic Allan Kozinn in a 2009 article, "Percussionists Go from Background to Podium." As reflected in his article, this is an exciting time to be a percussionist. The color palette of contemporary music has expanded drastically, and as a result, so has the role of the percussionist. No other instrument family equals percussion in coloristic variety and richness. Percussionists in professional settings have moved from background to forefront. With the greater role that percussionists now play comes a need for instructional materials that reflect this new reality. Teaching materials that once were based solely on a rudimentary model are no longer sufficient to prepare today's percussionist, who needs to be proficient in both pop and traditional genres, knowledgeable in world percussion styles, and expert in contemporary mallet percussion techniques.

Chris Colaneri has masterfully filled this need for pedagogical materials that prepare percussionists for the demands of the 21st century. With *Modern Etudes and Studies for the Total Percussionist*, Chris introduces students to skills not approached in other methods and does so in an organized, logical, and (most important) fun manner. The only thing left to say is: "Why are you still reading this introduction?" A world of percussion knowledge awaits you within the pages of this outstanding book, so get started, and don't forget to have fun!

Gary Mallinson
Artistic Director
Adventure Percussion

About the Companion Website

www.oup.com/us/thetotalpercussionist

This book comes with play-along tracks for accompanying all etudes and songs. I recommend rehearsing the etude or song first before trying to play along with the audio in order to work it up to tempo. These play-along tracks can be used not only as instructional material but also to accompany a performance, audition material for ensemble placement, and mid-term and final exams.

Demonstrating and explaining percussion instruments can be quite challenging. That is why at the beginning of each chapter there is a description of recommended techniques for a given instrument. To further assist with developing the correct techniques, each chapter has supplemental video tutorials. These videos and audio tracks can be found on the OUP website and are indicated in the text with this symbol ▶.

Introduction

Welcome to the world of TOTAL PERCUSSION! In this book you will find exercises and etudes that will instruct you in the six areas of percussion: snare drum, mallets, timpani, traps, drum set, and world percussion. There are also two percussion ensemble pieces at the end of the book that I hope you will enjoy.

The material in this book is an outgrowth of my experience as a percussion instructor and band director in the New York and New Jersey public school systems since 1996, as well as my private studies, which date back to 1983. It has always been my philosophy to create well-rounded percussion students who can play in any musical situation that comes their way. I have gone as far as to devote my master's studies to research what, why, and how percussion students are educated. Through this research, I concluded that band and percussion instructors needed and desired to prepare their students in this all-inclusive approach, but there was no culminating book to navigate through such a course of study. Previously, to prepare percussion students in the six areas of percussion, instructors needed six separate books. Not until now, with this book, has there been a comprehensive curriculum method that provides educational material that spans from the elementary through high school level.

My hope is that you will find the material in this book enjoyable and fun to play through. Please take your time and work through the material slowly so that you systematically build up a strong foundation. You will come to rely on this foundation as you call upon it to perform in your current and future music ensembles, in and beyond the school setting.

Equipment You Should Own

There are many demands performance ensembles place on the contemporary percussion student. The large number of colors and textures a percussionist is called to create requires the necessary tools to execute them. Keep in mind that the following equipment should be acquired over time. Ultimately, the necessary equipment a student should own depends on the teacher and the ensembles the student is involved in, as well as the student's budget. At various stages of development, percussion students should own the following mallets and equipment.

Some Basic Necessities
　　Practice Pad: The Real Feel 12-inch or the Remo practice pad
　　Metronome: Dr. Beat or a free downloadable app
　　Music Stand: On Stage SM7211

Elementary School
　　Drumsticks: Vic Firth 5A for fourth and fifth graders and 5B for sixth graders
　　　　and older
　　Bell/Xylophone Mallets: Malletech BB34 Bob Becker Series

Middle School

Snare Drumsticks (do not use on cymbals or drum set): Malletech Bob Becker BBSD and/or Michael Burritt MBSD (great for students who are taking auditions or want to create a full, mature sound for concert performance)

Drum Set Sticks: Vic Firth 5B (for rock drum set), Vic Firth 7A (for lighter jazz drumming)

Bell/Xylophone Mallets: Malletech BB34 Bob Becker Series

Often bell kits come with mallets. If you are using a Yamaha or Pearl bell kit, make sure that you get double-sided mallets; one side is a hard mallet for playing in a band, and the other is a soft side for practicing at home.

Bell Mallets: Malletech ESSB
Xylophone Mallets: Malletch BB34
Marimba Mallets: Malletech LS15 (1 pair)
Timpani Mallets: Malletech ESST medium

High School

High school percussionists keep adding to their tool boxes as they go. At this point, once you have the essentials in your stick bag, your mallet choices depend on the individual pieces you are performing.

Snare Drum Sticks: Malletech Bob Becker BBSD and/or Michael Burritt MBSD
Drum Set Sticks: Vic Firth 5A and 5B
Brushes: Vic Firth Heritage Brush Vic HB
Bell Mallets: Malletech ESSB
Xylophone Mallets: Malletech BB34 Bob Becker
Marimba Mallets: Malletech LS15 (two pair)
Timpani Mallets
Hard: Malletech ESHT
Medium: Malletech ESST
Soft: Malletech ESMT

Instruments and Equipment

Elementary School

Many schools have students purchase a bell and snare drum kit as a package. However, if you are purchasing individual instruments, I recommend the following.

Snare Drum: Pearl 12-by-5 Steel "Firecracker" Snare Drum (FCS1250)
Mallet Instrument: Percussion Adventure APX 2-Octave Xylophone
Metronome: Dr. Beat (although there are now many good apps on iPods that you can get free!)

Middle School

Usually by sixth or seventh grade, students have decided to commit themselves to percussion and are ready for their first drum set. I often get e-mails from parents asking what type of drum set I recommend. Ultimately, it comes down to price. I first recommend them to look on Craigslist but to be careful. The benefit of getting a drum set from Craigslist is that often it comes with all the hardware and cymbals. The drawback is that often the sets are a bit beat-up and all the heads need replacing. By the time you do that, it might have been worth just getting a new set. So I always recommend getting a new set if possible and buying a cymbal package. Parents always hesitate when it comes to buying a drum set, thinking that their child may not stick with it. I tell them that they can always sell it on Craigslist when they are done with it.

Drum Set: Yamaha Stage Custom Birch Bebop Shell Pack Drum Set or Pearl Export Series EXX705

Cymbal Package: Sabian SBR-2

Mallet Instrument: A bell kit at the middle-school level is fine, but the size of the bars is small, and it becomes more of a challenge to play as the student grows. I recommend a practice marimba (Musser M3PM) if it is in your budget.

High School

From this point forward, upgrading your equipment becomes a very personal choice. Often a private teacher gives the student direction, but here's my two cents.

Snare Drum: Pearl Philharmonic Snare Drum PHP (for the serious classical player)

Drum Set: Yamaha Stage Custom 22-inch bass drum (multiuse but mostly for rock)

Gretch Catalina Club Classic CC-J404 (jazz drumming)

Accessories for the Drum Set: Common add-ons for the set from Latin Percussion (LP) include Salsa, Cha Cha, and Mambo cowbells; mountable tambourines; and jam blocks.

Time to upgrade your cymbals? Personally, I like the Paiste Signature Series.

Marimba: Any entry level Malletech marimba or the Yamaha Acoutilon

Trap Percussion: tambourine (classical), Grover 10-inch double-row T2/HS; also recommended, Black Swamp 10-inch TD4S

Triangle: six-inch Alan Able; also recommended, Black Swamp six-inch Spectrum

Triangle Beaters: Stoessel Triangle Beater series

World Percussion

Congas: Pancho Sanchez by Remo

Bongos: Valencia by Remo

Timbales: Valencia by Remo

Djembes: I recommend the Remo 14-inch key tuned. There are many instruments on either end of the price range, and I suggest going to your local music store to try them out.

How to Use This Book

To teach all the aspects of total percussion within the course of a school year and make the most of this book, the music director has to organize the time allotted within the group lesson, as well as have a vision for the whole school year. If you have approximately a 44-minute lesson, you can teach two instrument groups for 22 minutes each and move students, as a group, between stations, for example, 22 minutes on mallets and 22 minutes on snare drum. Another model is having students at three different stations. In this scenario, if you had six students in a group, you would have two students practicing tambourine, two students practicing triangle, and two students practicing bass drum techniques. After 15 minutes, the students would rotate to a new station. As the teacher, you can make your rounds facilitating and demonstrating the appropriate techniques. Following are charts of how you might structure your school year to get through all the portions of this book. The ability level of your students will ultimately dictate how much can be accomplished within the lesson time, as well as how much material you will be able to cover within the school year.

Structuring the Year

Model 1A has three overlapping areas of study, with snare drum being the main focus, followed by mallets. Model 1B depicts how the lesson is disseminated throughout the school year. Model 2 is a quarterly approach in which two instruments are taught at the same time.

These charts show just some possible ways of structuring the year so that you can sequentially study all aspects of total percussion. They can be tailored to meet the needs of the music program, as well as the needs of the students. On the whole, the snare drum techniques provide a strong foundation that will transfer to all the other percussion instruments. That is why I recommend centering studies around the snare drum. Mallets would be the next focal point, followed by the timpani. Traps, drum set, and world percussion are very valuable areas of percussion study that, once mastered, can open up performance opportunities in the future. The important thing to remember is to approach total percussion with a game plan, or else it can be overwhelming.

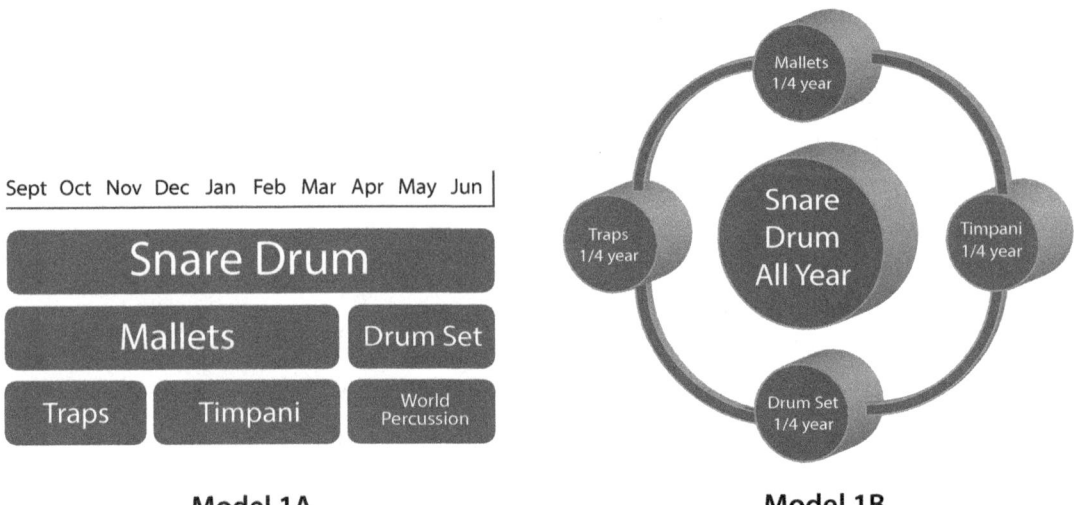

Model 1A

Model 1B

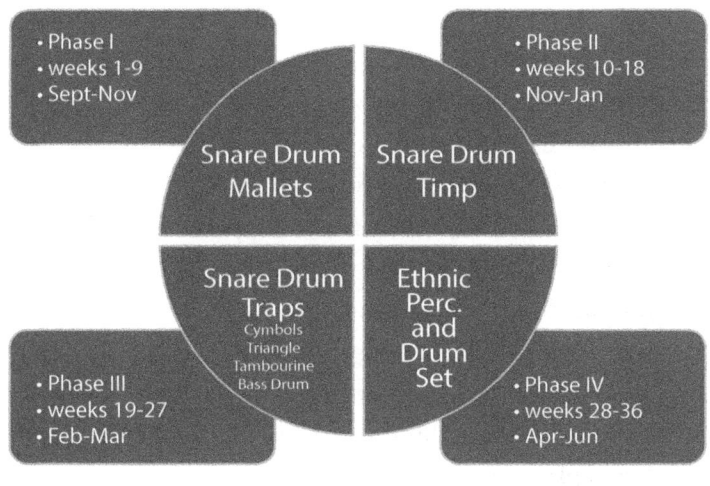

Model 2

About the Biography Section

At the end of each chapter are short biographies about famous percussionists. This section is intended to give you insight into the great musicians who set the stage for our current musical climate. These people are our ancestors who paved the way for us. If it wasn't for these percussionists, we wouldn't have the high standards we have today. Their voices shouted so loud that they commanded respect for percussion as an art form. The paths that they took to fame can, I hope, serve as a road map for your own career. Consider these biographies as a jumping-off point that inspires and motivates you to research more about their lives, accomplishments, and music.

How to Practice

The exercises in this book have been structured to meet the needs of the total percussion student. Studying percussion is vastly different from learning other instruments in that it requires the student to be proficient on multiple instruments within the percussion family. Organizing practice time and structuring the year to accommodate the six categories of percussion presented in this book take planning and foresight to see the full year in sections. Working with a qualified teacher helps students stay focused and attain the goals of the total percussionist.

Structuring Your Practice Time

One of the great life lessons that studying music offers is how to be organized and how to structure time to achieve a goal. For elementary and middle school students, I recommend practicing 30 to 45 minutes every other day. If you are motivated and driven and have the time to practice more, that would be great. You will improve that much faster.

First off, set aside a place in your home where you can practice and have room for all your percussion equipment. Next, set aside a practice time slot that the whole family knows is your time to play. Maybe a good time would be when your parents are elsewhere.

What should you practice first? I recommend, if you are a student who favors the snare drum or drum set, starting your practice session with a mallet instrument. If you start with the drums, you may run out of time at the end of your practice session to get to the mallets. If you favor the mallet instruments, then start with the drums.

When you start practicing, always begin with technique (scales, rudiments) and then etudes, and always set aside time for improvisation and experimenting with your instruments. You will be amazed with what you discover by just exploring your instrument in an unstructured way. One thing you can do is try to play melodies by ear on a mallet instrument. You can play along on the drum set to your favorite songs. These are valid and fun ways to practice that you will find exciting and motivational, but don't forget to keep the majority of your practice focused on technique and the etudes in this book. The skills required to perform these etudes are also the skills needed to play the music you love.

Some More Practice Ideas

Slow and steady wins the race. Be patient and consistent, and great things will come.

Practice right after your lesson so the material is fresh.

Practice with a metronome or play along with tracks that can be downloaded from the website ⏵.

Don't practice what you know. Practice what you need to improve.

Isolate the measure or group of notes that is giving you trouble, and repeat it over and over until you get it.

Get into a practice routine, such as right when you get home from school or after dinner.

Days one, three, and five, practice snare drum and mallets. On days two and four, practice other percussion instruments.

It's all right to practice in front of the TV. You can work on paradiddles and five-stroke rolls, but practice that requires more focus should be done in a space with no distractions.

From my years of teaching and from having children of my own, I know how hard it is to set aside time to practice. There are so many outside obligations, from sports to religious school to playing with friends to doing homework, that can take you away from practicing. Once you commit yourself and set aside a practice routine, you are going to be amazed at how much you will grow as a musician.

Practice Assignment Sheet

Date	Assignment	Sun	Mon	Tues	Wed	Thur	Fri	Sat	Parent's Initials	Grade

Practice Assignment Sheet

Date	Assignment	Sun	Mon	Tues	Wed	Thur	Fri	Sat	Parent's Initials	Grade

Modern Etudes and Studies
for the Total Percussionist

Staff Attributes

Staff: The five lines and four spaces music is written on.

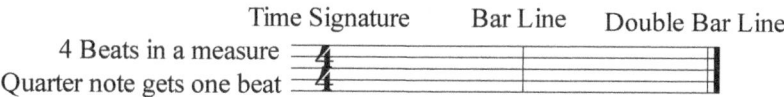

Staff   Measure

Measure: Space where music is written.

Time signature:

Top number: Number of beats in a measure.

Time Signature   Bar Line   Double Bar Line

4 Beats in a measure

Quarter note gets one beat

Bottom number: Tells what note gets what beat.

Bar lines: Separate measures.

Double bar line: Shows the end of a section or end of the song.

Elements of Music

Clef: Places a note on the staff.

Treble Clef: Five lines: E G B D F; four spaces: F A C E.

Treble or G Clef

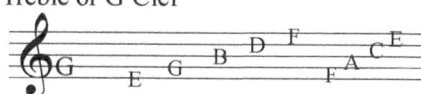

Bass Clef: Five lines: G B D F A; four spaces: A C E G.

Bass or F Clef

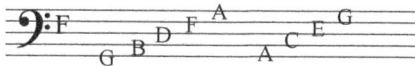

Neutral Clef: A nonpitched clef.

Neutral Celf (a non-pitch celf)

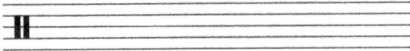

Repeat Signs

Repeat Signs: Tell instrumentalist to go back and replay a section.

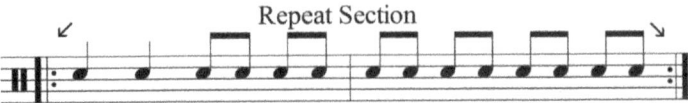

One-Bar Repeat Sign: Repeat previous measure.

Two-Bar Repeat Sign: Repeat previous two measures.

First and Second Ending: When playing a song, play into the first ending and follow repeat. The second time you play the passage, skip the first ending and proceed to the second ending.

Segno: Sign.

Coda: Ending section of a musical work.

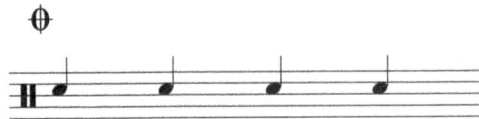

Fine: End of musical work.

Fine

D.S. al coda: To the sign and play to the coda.

D.S. al Coda

D.C. al coda: To the top (*capo*) and play to the coda.

D.S. al fine: Go to the sign and follow to fine.

D.S. al Fine

D.C. al fine: To the top and play to fine.

D.C. al Fine

Rhythm Table

Note Names, Rests, and Values in 4/4 Time

WHOLE	o	▬	4 BEATS
HALF	♩	▬	2 BEATS
QUARTER	♩	;	1 BEAT
EIGHTH	♪	،	½ BEAT
SIXTEENTH	♬	;	¼ BEAT

Accidentals

Flat (♭): Lowers a note by a haltf step.

Sharp (♯): Raises a note by a half step.

Natural (♮): Cancels the previous sharp or flat and returns the note to its original pitch.

Dynamics and Stick Height

Dynamics in relationship to stick height is not an exact science. Dynamics are dependent on two main factors: the size of the room you are playing in and the number of performers you are playing with. The larger the group and the bigger the room, the louder your dynamics will be.

FORTISSISSIMO	*fff*	VERY, VERY STRONG	THREE-QUARTER (67 DEGREES) OR FULL STROKE (90 DEGREES)
FORTISSIMO	*ff*	VERY STRONG	THREE-QUARTER (67 DEGREES) OR FULL STROKE (90 DEGREES)
FORTE	*f*	STRONG	THREE-QUARTER STROKE (67 DEGREES)
MEZZO FORTE	*mf*	MEDIUM STRONG	HALF STROKE (45–50 DEGREES)
MEZZO PIANO	*mp*	MEDIUM SOFT	HALF STROKE (40 DEGREES)
PIANO	*p*	SOFT	QUARTER STROKE (20 DEGREES)
PIANISSIMO	*pp*	VERY SOFT	QUARTER STROKE (10 DEGREES)
PIANISSISSIMO	*ppp*	VERY, VERY SOFT	QUARTER STROKE (5 DEGREES)

Accent: Play note stronger.

Staccato: Play note shorter (half the note value).

Crescendo: Gradually get louder.

Decrescendo: Gradually get softer.

Full Stroke

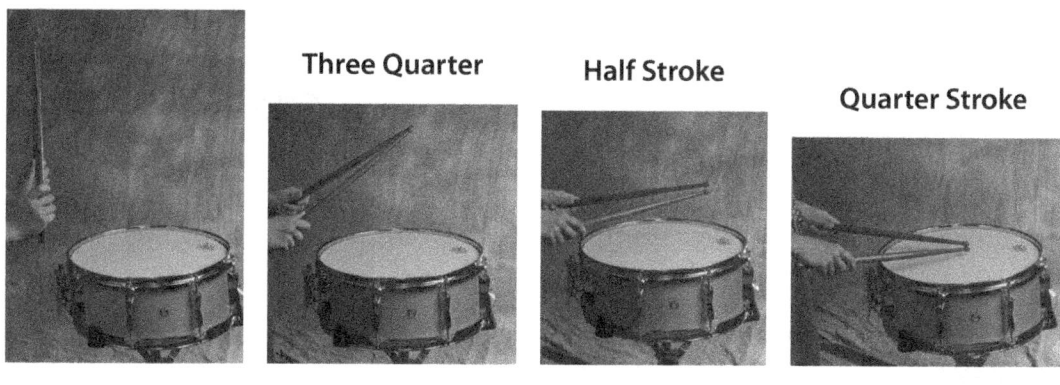

Three Quarter

Half Stroke

Quarter Stroke

Most playing will be done at the half-stroke level. The full stroke should be reserved for fortissimo playing and for certain warm-ups on a practice pad.

Tempos and Metronome Marking

LENTO	SLOW	40–45 BPM
LARGO	BROAD	45–50 BPM
ADAGIO	SLOW AND STATELY	55–65 BPM
ANDANTE	WALKING PACE	73–77 BPM
MODERATO	MODERATE	86–97 BPM
ALLEGRO	FAST, QUICKLY	109–132 BPM
VIVACE	LIVELY AND FAST	132–140 BPM
PRESTO	EXTREMELY FAST	150 AND UP!

http://en.wikipedia.org/wiki/Tempo
BPM: Beats per minute.

Altering Tempos

Accelerando: Gradually accelerate.
Ritardando: Gradually slow down.

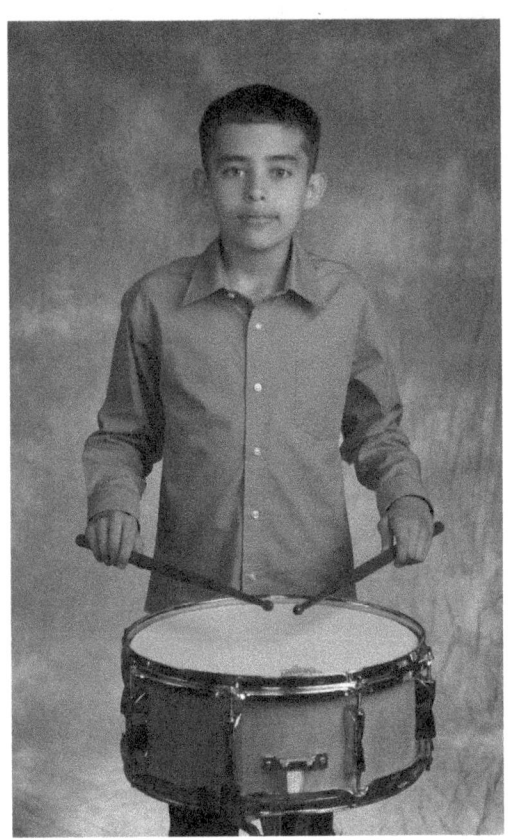

Setup and Stance

Set snare drum at waist height with the snare strainer release facing toward you. Your body should be about three inches from the drum. Your feet should be spaced about a foot apart, and your arms should bend at a 65-degree angle from the elbow.

Holding the Sticks

1. Grip sticks with thumb and index finger approximately two and a half inches from the back of the stick.
2. Loosely wrap remaining fingers around stick.
3. Palm faces floor with sticks in a V formation.
4. Middle finger sets sticks in motion, along with the wrist and slight movement of the arm.
5. The ring finger and pinky are also used to drive the stick to the head of the snare drum.
6. When lowering the stick to the head, let the stick rebound off the head so that the stick bounces back to its original height.
7. Beating spot should be slightly off-center above the snare bed.
8. For soft dynamics, play low and toward the edge of the drum.

Video 2.1: SD Grip and Stroke ▶

Rolls

To develop a good closed concert roll, you will need to develop a good buzz stroke by each stick. In exercise 2 on the next page, the buzz is represented by three slashes through the stem of the note. When practicing buzz exercises, make sure that each buzz sustains into the next buzz. There should be no silence between buzzed notes.

Video 2.2: Rolls ▶

Warm-up Exercises and Rudiments

Rate Changers

Exercise 1

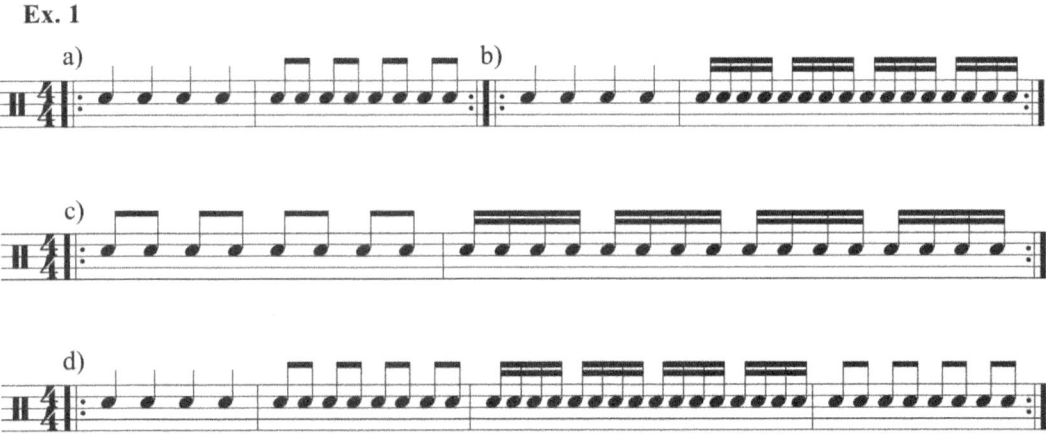

Buzz Exercises

Buzz one stick into the head at a time.

Exercise 2

Roll Exercises

The Long Roll

Measured Roll Exercises

Five-Stroke Roll

Seven-Stroke Roll

Nine-Stroke Roll

Paradiddles

a) Single

R L R R L R L L

b) Double

R L R L R R L R L R L L

c) Triple

R L R L R L R R L R L R L R L L

Video 2.3: Paradiddles ▶

Flam Exercises

a) Single Flam

l R r L l R r L

b) Flam Tap

l R R r L L l R R r L L

c) Flam Accent

lR L R rL R L lR L R rL R L

Video 2.4: Flams ▶

d) Flamacue

lR L R L   lR   rL R L R   rL

e) Flam Paradiddle

lR   L   R   R   rL   R   L   L

Drag Exercises

a) Single Drag

l l R   r r L   l l R   r r L

b) Drag Tap

l l R   L   r r L   R   l l R   L   r r L   R

c) Lesson 25

ll R L R ll R L R ll R L R ll R L R

d) Single Ratamacue

l l R L R L r r L R L R   l l R L R L r r L R L R

e) Single Stroke Ruff

l r l R   l r l R   l r l R   l r l R

Video 2.5: Drags ▶

Accent Patterns

16th-Note Accent Patterns

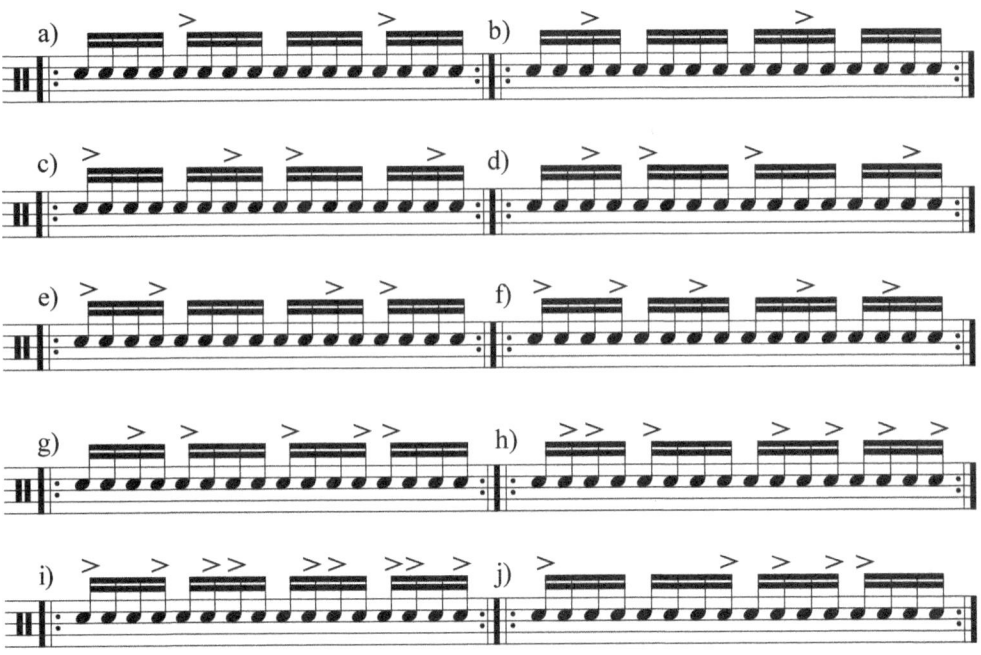

Triplet Accent Patterns

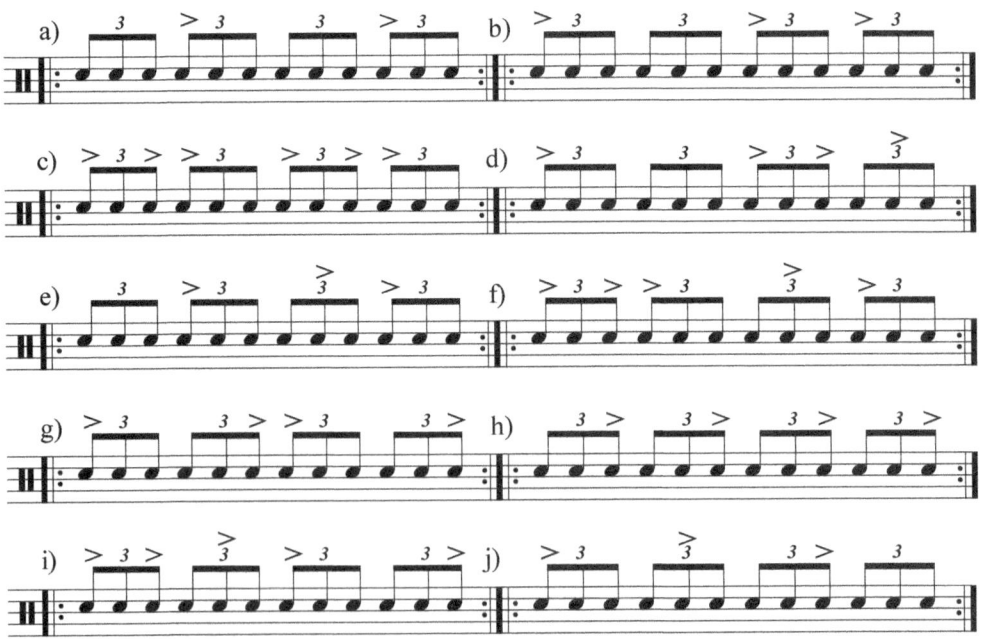

It's recommended for students to write their own accent patterns. Once mastered on the snare drum, they can be applied as fills or solo ideas around the drum set.

Sticking Patterns

Eighth-Note Sticking Patterns

Triplet Sticking Patterns

Right-Hand Lead

This technique has the performer play the right-hand strokes on the strong beats of a measure. This allows the player to phrase to the beat and is often a more comfortable sticking to execute. This technique can apply to students who are left-handed just by reversing the sticking. Some teachers promote the alternate stroke concept, which develops the hands equally. In this approach, the player alternates sticking regardless of rhythm. The best way to understand the two techniques is to practice the following exercises before each rhythm is introduced throughout the book. Column A represents the alternate sticking approach, and column B shows the same rhythm using right-hand lead.

R L R L R L R R L R R L

R L R L R R R L L R

R L R L R L L R

R LRL RLR LRL RL R RLR RLR RLR RL

RLR LRL RLR LRL LRL LRL LRL LRL

RL RLR LRL RLR L RL LRL LRL LRL L

R L R L R L R L L L L L L L L L

Rhythm Studies

Play through exercises 1 and 2 using the full, half, and quarter stroke.

16

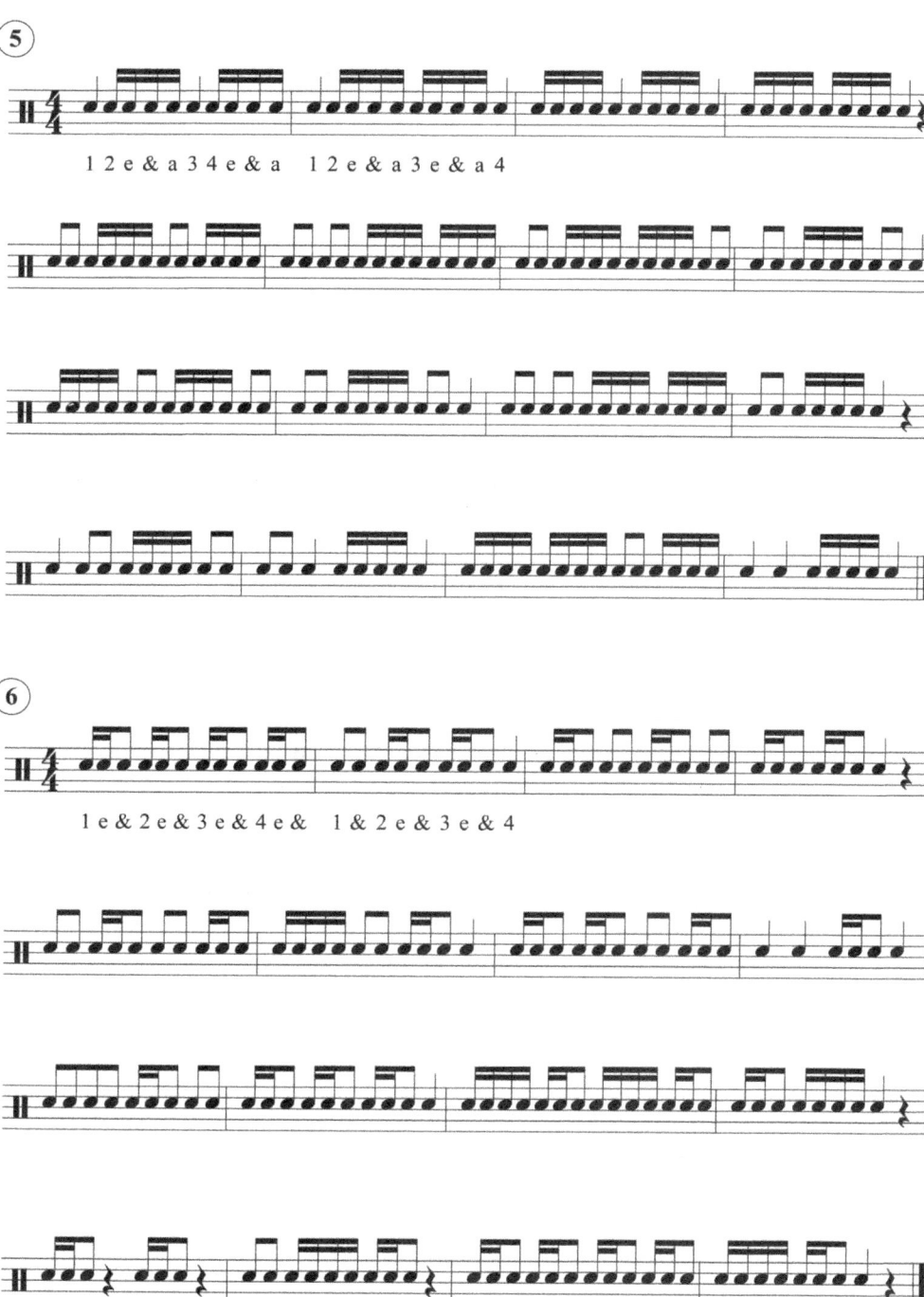

18

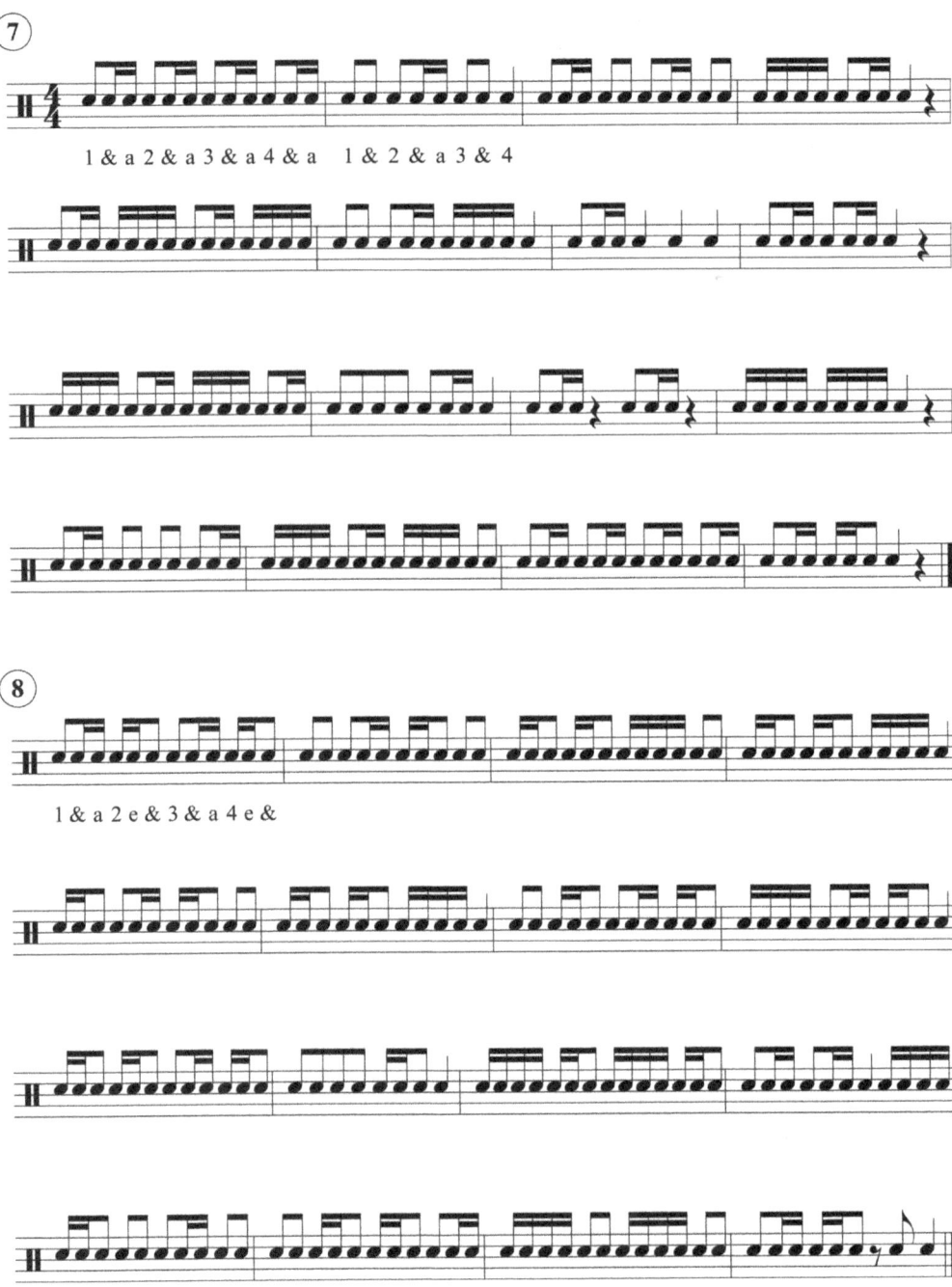

In exercise 11, the concept of syncopation is introduced. When a quarter note lands on an ampersand (&), it takes up the space of the & plus the number that follows. That is because a quarter note contains two eighth notes. When a single eighth note lands on a down beat or number, the next available space to place a note is on the &. You can write in the numbers below the staff to help you keep your place.

If all else fails, think of this exercise in terms of long-short rhythms. For a quarter note, say and play long, and for an eighth note, say and play short.

Putting It All Together

Advanced Rhythms

1

1 e a 2 & 3 e a 4 &

2

e & a   e & a   e & a   e & a

3

e &   e &   e &   e &

4

R R R R R R   R L R L R L

Roll Studies

Rolls on the eighth note can first be played as five-stroke rolls and then as seven-stroke rolls at a slower tempo.

Snare Drum Etudes

Quarter, Eighth, and Sixteenth

Preliminary Warm-up

17-Stroke Roll   **32-Stroke Roll**

1e&a 2e&a   3   1e&a 2e&a 3e&a 4e&a 1

I

Track 2.1

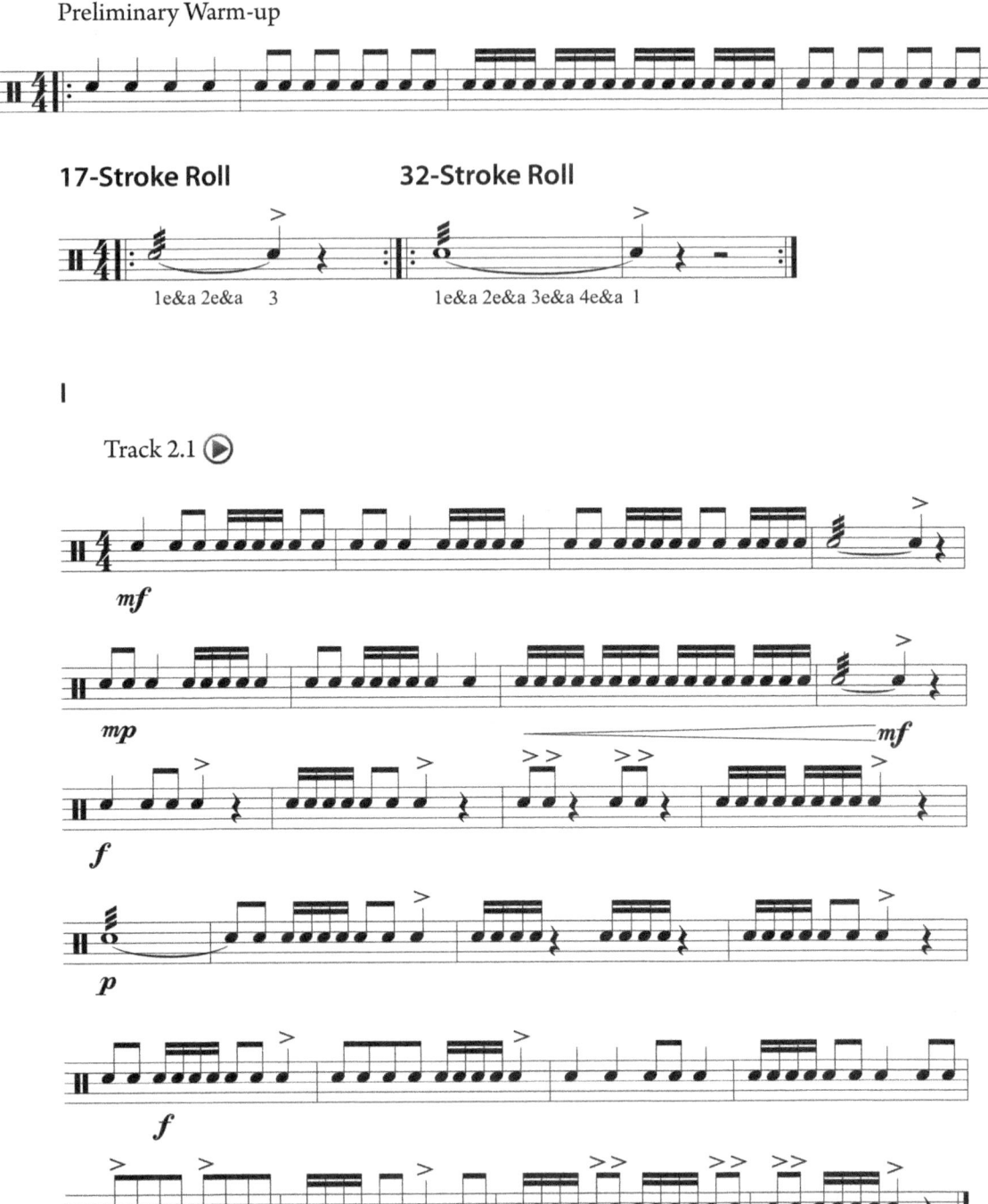

Eighth-Note Rests

Preliminary Warm-up

Flam

9 Stroke Roll

II

Track 2.2 ▶

Eighth-Note Triplets

Preliminary Warm-up

Lines 1–3

Flam Tap

lR R rL L lR R rL L

III

Track 2.3 ▶

Ties and Dots

Preliminary Warm-up

1 & 2 & 3 & 4 &   1 & 2 & 3 & 4 &   1 & 2 & 3 & 4 &

1 & 2 & 3 & 4 &   1 & 2 & 3 & 4 &   1 & 2 & 3 & 4 &

1 & 2 & 3 & 4 &   1 & 2 & 3 & 4 &   1 & 2 & 3 & 4 &

Drag

l l R   rr L   l l R   rr L

IV

Track 2.4 ▶

1E&, 1E

Preliminary Warm-up

Five-Stroke Roll

Lesson 25

R L R L R L R L R L R L   ‖ R L R ‖ R L R ‖ R L R ‖ R L R

V

Track 2.5 ▶

1&A, &A

Preliminary Warm-up

Single Paradiddle

Five-Stroke Roll

VI

Track 2.6 ▶

Students can play all 16th notes as paradiddles.

1 A

Preliminary Warm-up

RRLRRLRRLRRL R LR LR LR L RLRLRLRL

Four-Stroke Ruff

l r l R   r l r L   l r l R   r l r L

VII

Track 2.7 ▶

Odd Time: 6/8

Preliminary Warm-up

Flam Accent   ### Double Paradiddle

lR L R rL R L   R L R L R R L R L R L L

VIII

Track 2.8 ▶

Students can play double paradiddle where applicable.

16th-Note Triplets

Preliminary Warm-up

Ratamacue

Seven-Stroke Roll

l l R L R L   r r L R L R   l l R L R L   r r L R L R   R l r l R l r l R lrl R lrl R

IX

Track 2.9 ▶

Cut Time/Alla Breve

Preliminary Warm-up

1 2 3 4   1 & 2 &   1 & 2 & 3 & 4 &   1 e & a 2 e & a

1   3   1   2   1 2 3 4   1   2

Flamacue

Syncopation

Preliminary Warm-up

XI

Track 2.11

Swing Time

Preliminary Warm-up (b and c should be played the same way)

XII

Track 2.12

More 16th-Note Variations

E&A

Preliminary Warm-up

1 e & a 2 e & a 3 e & a 4 e & a   1 e & a 2 e & a 3 e & a 4 e & a

Flam Paradiddle

lR L R R rL R L L lR L R R rL R L L

XIII

Track 2.13 ▶

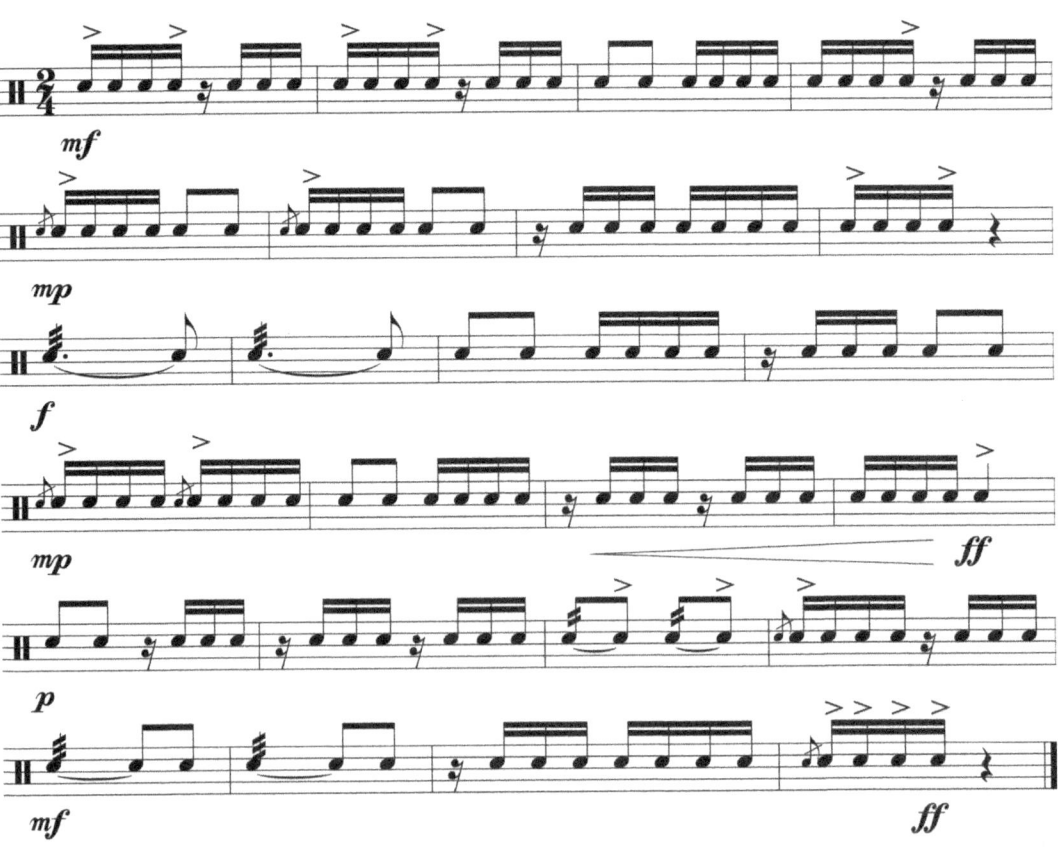

1 E A

Preliminary Warm-up

Drag Tap

XIV

Track 2.14 ▶

E &

Preliminary Warm-up

1   e   &   a   2   e   &   a   3   e   &   a   4   e   &   a

e &   e &   e &   e &   e &   e &   e &   e &

XV

Track 2.15 ▶

E A

Preliminary Warm-up

e a e a e a e a   ea ea ea ea

XVI

Track 2.16 ▶

Quarter-Note and Broken-up Triplets

Preliminary Warm-up

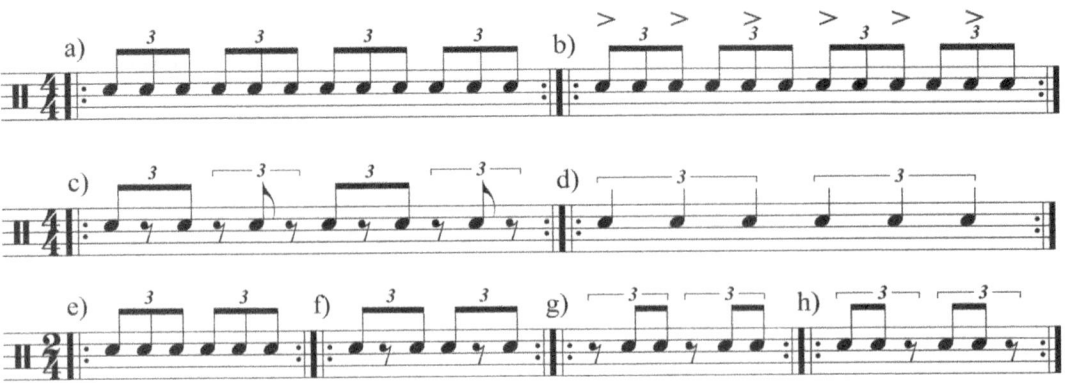

XVII

Track 2.17 ▶

Advanced Odd-Time Signatures

Preliminary Warm-up

Time Travel
(Odd-Time Solo)

XVIII

Advanced Swing Solo

XIX

Once this solo is learned on the snare drum, you can place the rhythms around the drum set. Play quarter notes softly on the bass drum, and have the hi-hat play on two and four with your foot.

Rudimental Solo

XX

Percussionist Spotlight: Snare Drum

Buster Bailey

1922–2004

Elden Chandler "Buster" Bailey performed with the New York Philharmonic for 40 years and taught at the prestigious Julliard School for more than 20 years. During his tenure with the New York Philharmonic, he performed under Leonard Bernstein and in most major cities around the world. As an educator, Buster is known for his acclaimed snare drum book, *Wrist Twisters*. Many of his students play in major orchestras around the world, and his snare drum technique is still taught today.

In high school, Buster was known more for his xylophone playing. It is said that he gave more than 100 concerts on xylophone before finishing high school. After high school, Bailey went to the New England Conservatory of Music but halted his schooling to serve in the Army during World War II. Afterward, he went to Julliard as a student and freelanced for commercials, symphonies, and many recording dates. In 1949, his former teacher recommended him to audition for the New York Philharmonic, and the rest is history.

Anthony J. Cirone

1941–

From Jersey City, N.J., Anthony J. Cirone is most noted for his snare drum etude book, *Portraits in Rhythm*. This book is used in most colleges and universities throughout the world. Cirone attended the Julliard School for his undergraduate degree, as well as his master's. After his studies, he went on to perform with the San Francisco Symphony for 36 years. In this position, he worked under such great conductors as Leonard Bernstein, Seiji Ozowa, Igor Stravinsky, Aaron Copland, and Kurt Masur.

Over the years, Cirone has been affiliated with many colleges and universities. He has held positions at San Jose State University, San Francisco State University, Stanford University, and the Jacobs School of Music at Indiana. Among percussionists, he is well respected and has won the *Modern Drummer*'s Readers Poll as best classical percussionist for five years in a row.

KEYBOARD PERCUSSION 3

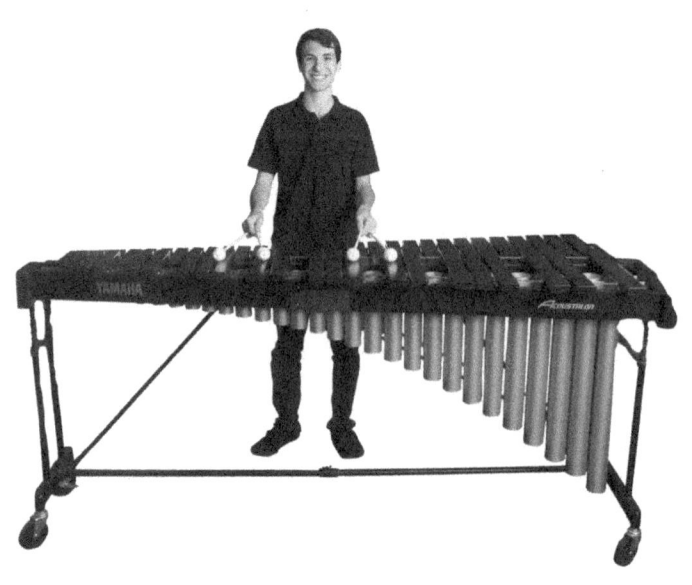

The main keyboard percussion instruments of the percussion family are the orchestra bells, xylophone, chimes, vibes, and marimba.

Keyboard Geography

Memorizing where the notes are on a mallet instrument can be challenging and takes time to master. Once you feel comfortable with bar recognition, applying the notes on the staff to your mallet instrument will become easier. The following diagram gives you the note placement on all mallet instruments:

Marimba Graphic with Chromatic Notes

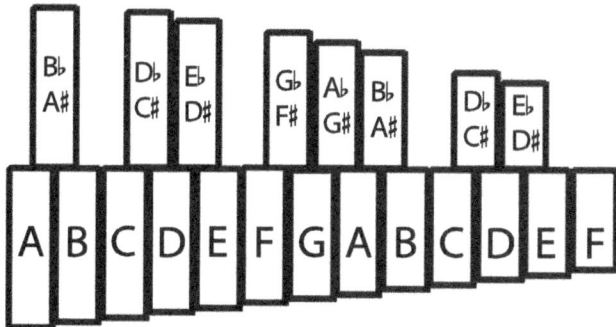

Half Step: The distance from one note to the next consecutive note (up or down) without any skips.

Whole Step: Two half steps in any direction.

Accidentals: Alterations to a note that either raise or lower a pitch.

Sharp: Raises a note by a half step and is represented by a number sign, ♯.

Flat: Lowers a note by a half step and is represented by the flat symbol ♭ that looks like a low-ercase letter b.

Natural Sign: Cancels the previous sharp or flat and returns the note to its original pitch. This symbol is represented as follows: ♮

Diatonic Intervals: The distance between notes within a scale.

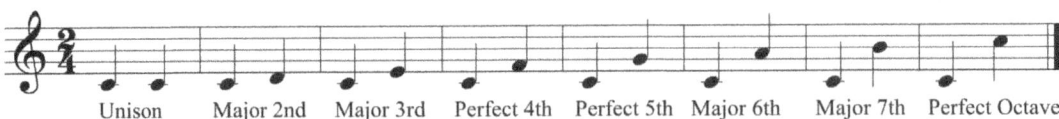

Unison Major 2nd Major 3rd Perfect 4th Perfect 5th Major 6th Major 7th Perfect Octave

Chromatic Intervals: The distance between notes of the chromatic scale.

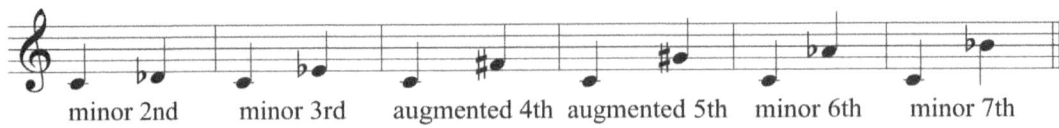

minor 2nd minor 3rd augmented 4th augmented 5th minor 6th minor 7th

The Chromatic Scale

Scale Construction

Here are the patterns used to create the major and minor scales. Practice starting on different notes to create any major or minor scale of your choice.

Whole Step = W

Half Step = H

Major Scale Construction: W W H W W W H.

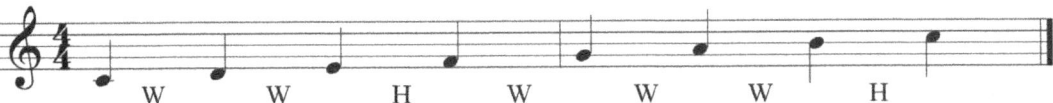

W W H W W W H

Natural Minor Scale Construction: W H W W H W W.

W H W W H W W

Posture: Always stand between the highest and lowest note that you are going to play in the music. Keep your feet and legs balanced, and shift your weight toward the note you are playing.

Holding Your Mallets

Hold your mallets the way you would when you play snare drum.

Slightly rotate your wrists outward. Because a mallet bar does not have the rebound of a snare drum, use your wrist to give a slight lift to the mallet after striking the bar in order to bring out the tone.

Beating Spots

The best beating spot on the marimba is in the center of the bar over the resonators. The next best beating spot on the raised bars is on the edge toward the lower bars. Never play over the strings (node) or screws. This creates a thin and undesirable tone.

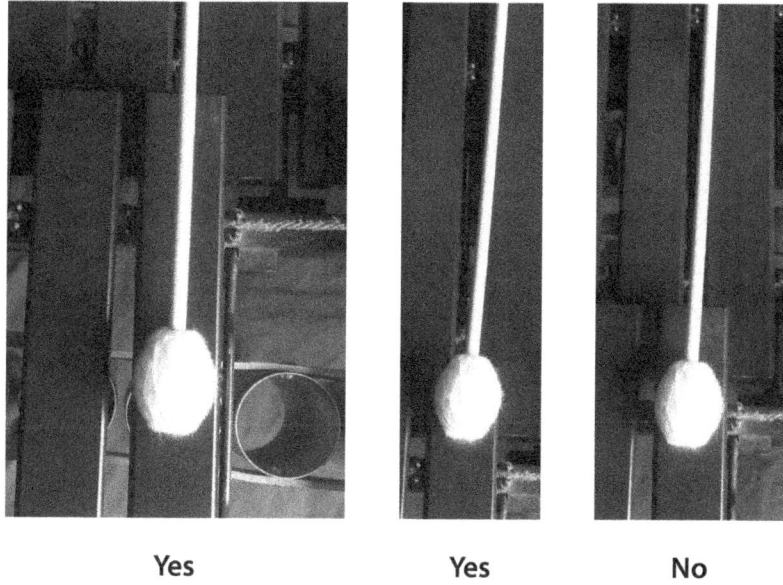

| **Yes** | **Yes** | **No** |

Peripheral Vision: When playing these exercises, be sure not to memorize the notes and then play them. Do your best to use your peripheral vision to see the notes and the bars at the same time. You can use the raised bars as a reference point for finding notes.

Remember that it is better to a hit wrong note and keep your place in the music than it is to memorize the notes and look down to strike them. Some teachers use the look up/look down technique. This is OK to use when you are just beginning.

The Rule of Motion: If the notes ascend up the staff from line to space or space to line, your mallets move to the right without skipping a bar.

If the notes move down the staff in the same manner, move your mallets to the left of your instrument.

If notes on the staff move from line to line or space to space, leave a bar between the notes you strike. This single bar skip is called an interval of a third. This skip is used in the first three notes of the arpeggio.

A double bar skip is when a note moves from a line and passes the next line and is placed on the next space. This is called an interval of a fourth (Ex. 8). A double bar skip can also start on a space, pass the next space, and be placed on the next line. These skips can be seen between the third and fourth notes of an arpeggio.

Rolls

Single-stroke rolls are to be played when rolling on a mallet instrument. On the roll exercises, do not break roll. Keep your hands in motion while changing notes.

Percussion Ensemble Arrangements

The songs in this section can easily be turned into percussion ensemble arrangements by having one person play the chord changes on marimba, piano, or even guitar. Another person can play the roots on bass or keyboards or the low end of a marimba. Drum set and world percussion instruments can be added to fill out the sound. The arrangement can deviate from the written music by adding drum solos and percussion breaks.

Video 3.1: Mallet Grip and Beating Spots ▶

Video 3.2: Rolls ▶

Each song on the play-along tracks has a four-bar intro.

My First Notes!

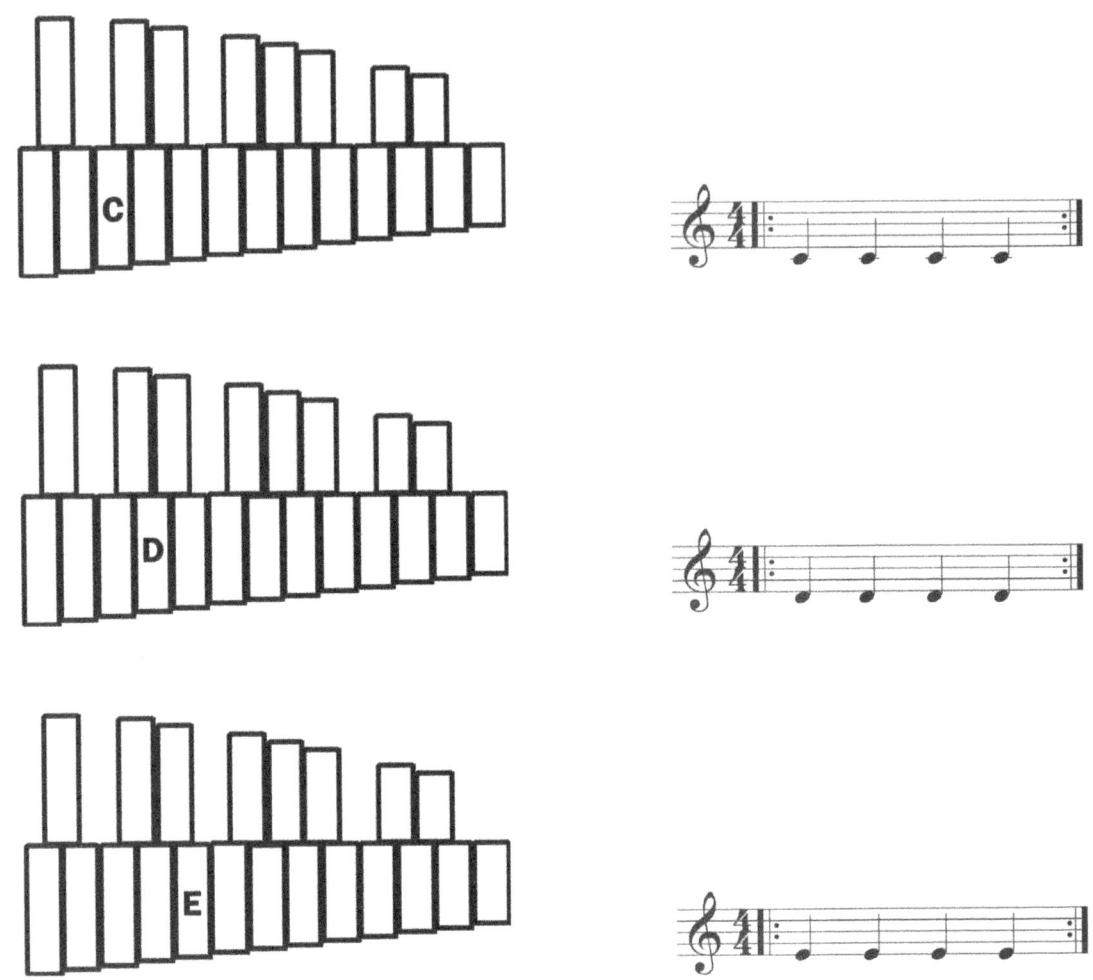

Three-note combination say-n-play.

C D E

Alternate hands from right to left.

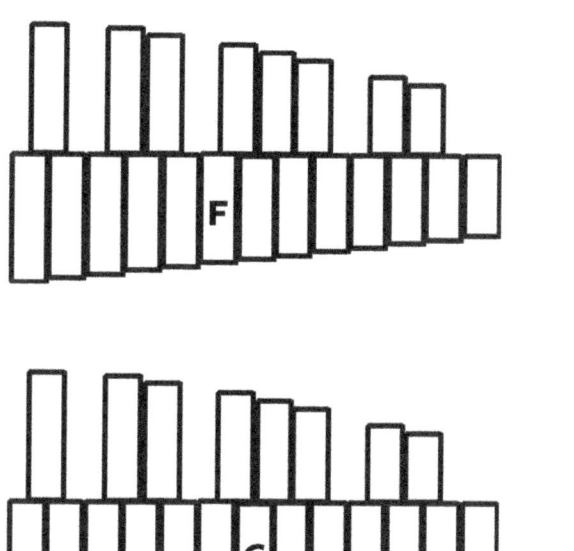

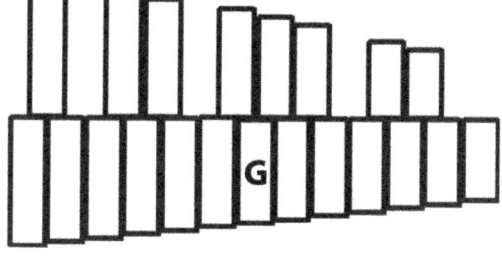

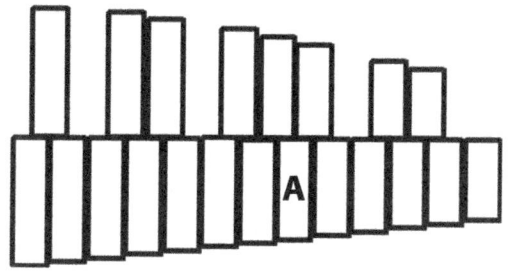

Three-note combination say-n-play.

F G A

Alternate hands from right to left.

My First Notes (continued)

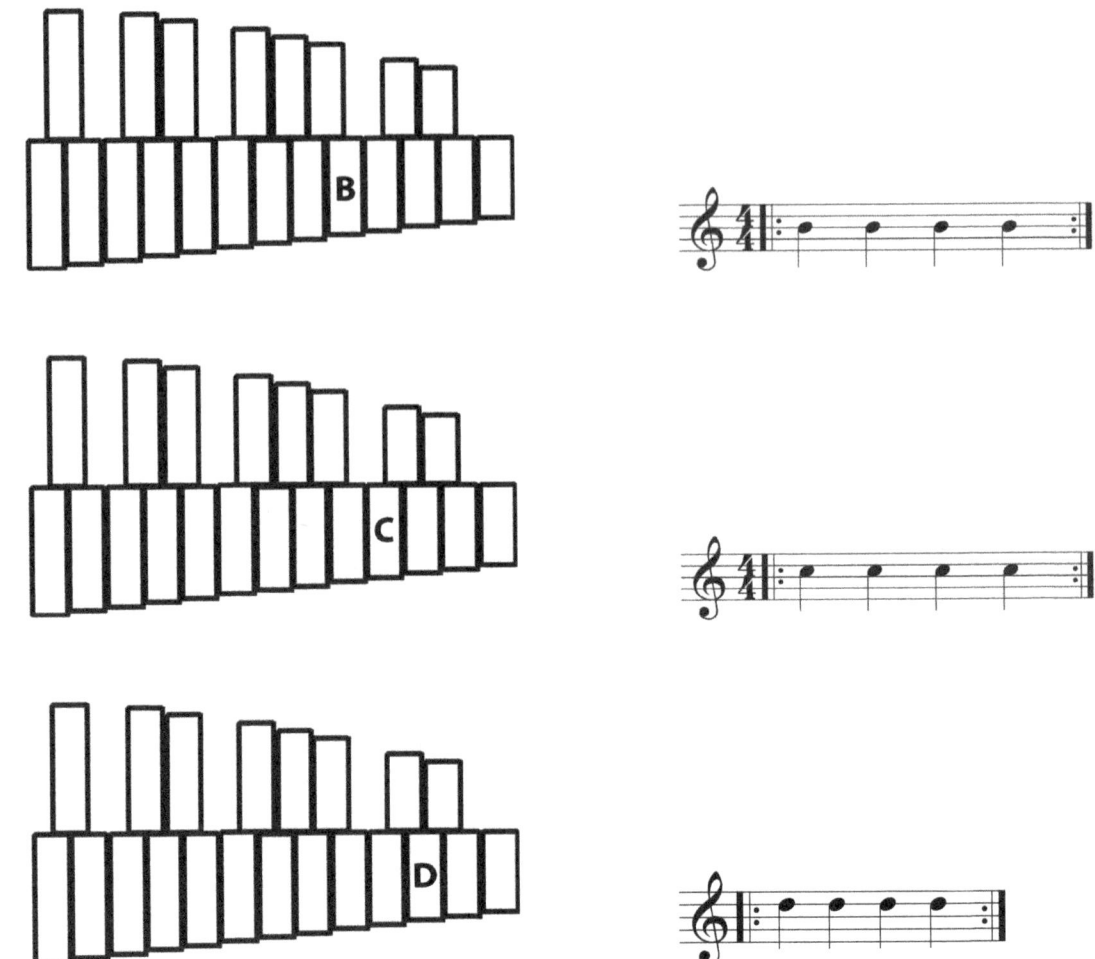

Three-note combination say-n-play.

B C D

Alternate hands from right to left.

Preliminary Mallet Exercises

Say or sing notes while you play.

Say-n-Plays C Major

Say the names of the notes out loud while you play. Repeat each measure until you are comfortable naming the notes. Alternate sticking from right to left.

Just a Few Short Melodies

America

Ward

My Country 'Tis of Thee

English Traditional

Yankee Doodle

Hopkinson

Frère Jacques

French Traditional

Jingle Bells

Pierpont

When Irish Eyes Are Smiling

Ball

Amazing Grace

English Traditional

Camptown Races

Foster

Say-n-Plays B♭ Major

Below is a say-n-play exercise in the key of B♭. Some teachers like to start their mallet students in this key because much of the beginning concert band literature is in B♭. Once you master these say-n-plays, you can proceed to the B♭ scale studies and melodies in this book.

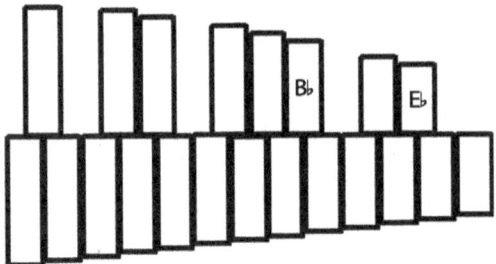

Techniques Building and Melodies

C Major

Five-Note Scale

Eight-Note Scale

C Major Scale

Eighth-Note Twisters

Triplet Twisters

Rhythm Study

Extended Range

Movement in Thirds

Arpeggios

A Natural Minor Scale

A Harmonic Minor Scale

A Melodic Minor Scale

61

Four Seasons

Track 3.1 audio

Adagio

Vivaldi

African Welcome Song

Track 3.2 audio

Moderato

African Traditional

Fly Me Home

Track 3.3 audio

Andante

Colaneri

*Play first time only

All songs play three times with a four-bar intro.

On The Island

(Unaccompanied Mallet Solo)

Presto

Colaneri

B♭ Major

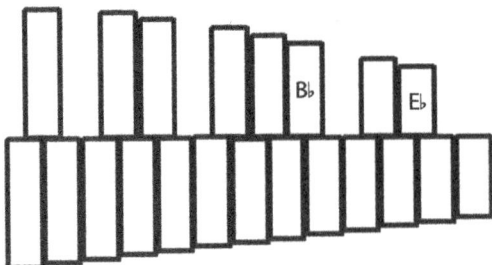

A flat lowers a note by a half step.

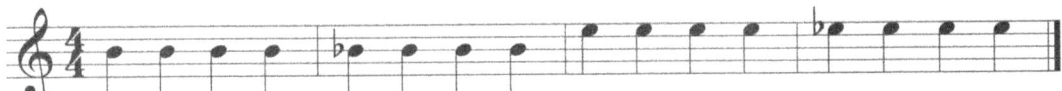

Five-Note Scale

Mixing It Up

Rolls

Twisters

Crazy Twisters

B♭ Major Scale

Eighth-Note Twisters

Triplet Twisters

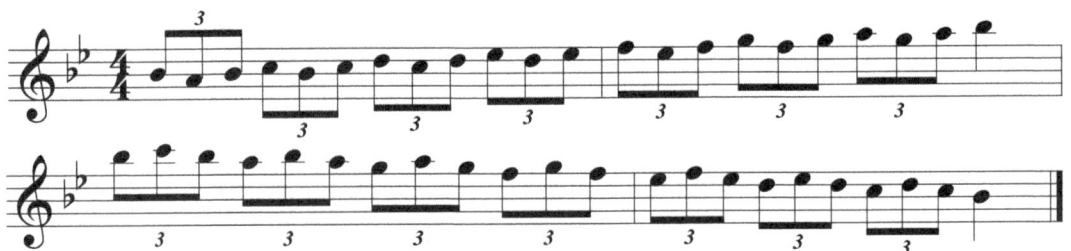

Rhythm Check: Ties

Extended Range

Accidentals

Movement in Thirds

Arpeggios

G Natural Minor Scale

G Harmonic Minor Scale

G Melodic Minor Scale

Sonata #1

Track 3.4 ▶

Andante   **Mozart**

Linstead Market

(Form: AABA)

Track 3.5 ▶

Moderato   **Island Traditional**

Don't Be Blue Monk

Track 3.6

Andante   Colaneri

Vallant

(Unaccompanied Mallet Solo)

Allegro   Colaneri

F Major

F Major Scale

Eighth-Note Twisters

Triplet Twisters

Rhythm Check: 1&A

F Blues Scale

Movement in Thirds

Arpeggios

D Natural Minor Scale

D Harmonic Minor Scale

D Melodic Minor Scale

Sonata in F

Track 3.7 ▶

Allegro

Handel

Tingalayo

Track 3.8 ▶

Moderato

Island Traditional

Now's Not the Time

Track 3.9

Andante

Colaneri

Sprite

(Unaccompanied Mallet Solo)

Andante

Colaneri

G Major

Introducing F♯

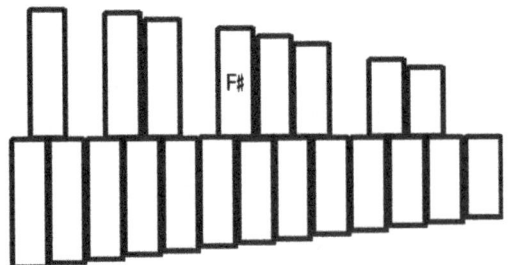

A sharp raises a note by a half step.

G Major Scale

Eighth-Note Twisters

Triplet Twisters

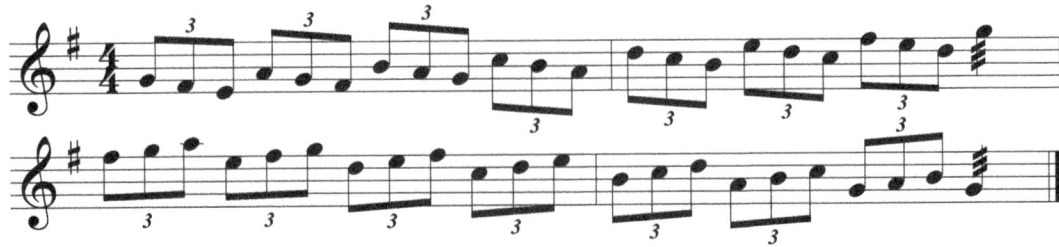

Rhythm Check: Dotted Quarters

Movement in Thirds

G Blues Scale

Arpeggios

E Natural Minor Scale

E Harmonic Minor Scale

E Melodic Minor Scale

Eine Kleine Nachtmusik

Track 3.10 ▶

Presto

Mozart

La Cucaracha

Track 3.11 ▶

Moderato

Mexican Traditional

G Jam Blues

Track 3.12 ▶

Andante   Colaneri

Smile

(Unaccompanied Mallet Solo)

Allegro   Colaneri

D Major

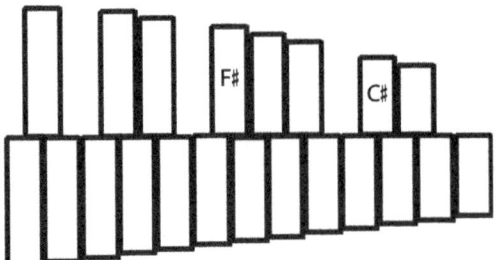

Introducing C#

D Major Scale

Eighth-Note Twisters

Triplet Twisters

Rhythm Check: 1E&

79

Movement in Thirds

Arpeggios

B Natural Minor Scale

B Harmonic Minor Scale

B Melodic Minor Scale

Dance of the Tumblers

Track 3.13 ▶

Presto

Rimsky-Korsakov

White Dove

Track 3.14 ▶

Moderato

Colaneri

Cotton Doll

Track 3.15

Andante

Colaneri

Triumph
(Unaccompanied Mallet Solo)

Allegro

Colaneri

E♭ Major

Introducing A♭

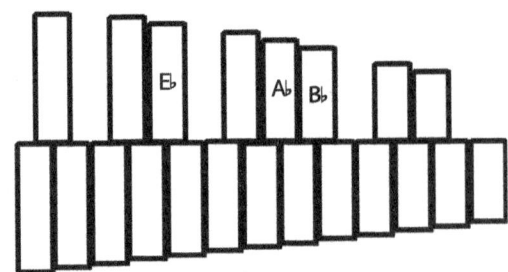

E♭ Major Scale

Eighth-Note Twisters

Triplet Twisters

Rhythm Check: 1 A

Movement in Thirds

Arpeggios

C Natural Minor Scale

C Harmonic Minor Scale

C Melodic Minor Scale

Nutcracker March

Track 3.16 ▶

Presto

Tchaikovsky

La Bamba

Track 3.17 ▶

Vivace

Mexican Traditional

Red Bossa

Track 3.18

Moderato

Colaneri

Momentum

(Unaccompanied Mallet Solo)

Presto

Colaneri

A Major

Introducting G♯

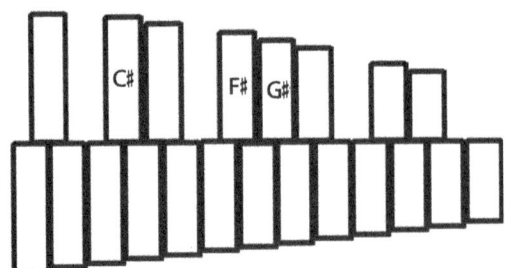

A Major Scale

Eighth-Note Twisters

Triplet Twisters

Rhythm Check: 1EA

Movement in Thirds

Arpeggios

F♯ Natural Minor Scale

F♯ Harmonic Minor Scale

F♯ Melodic Minor Scale

Carmen

Track 3.19 ▶

Andante

Bizet

Sly Mongoose

Track 3.20 ▶

Presto

Jamaican Traditional

Ahey Train

Track 3.21

Allegro

Colaneri

Set Sail

(Unaccompanied Mallet Solo)

Presto

Colaneri

Further Scale Studies

At this point in your studies, you probably have an understanding that scales are made up of visual patterns on the keyboard. As you play through these scales and patterns, improvise your own exercises using each key signature.

For example, play diatonically up three notes and back one, or play through the scale in thirds, fourths, and fifths.

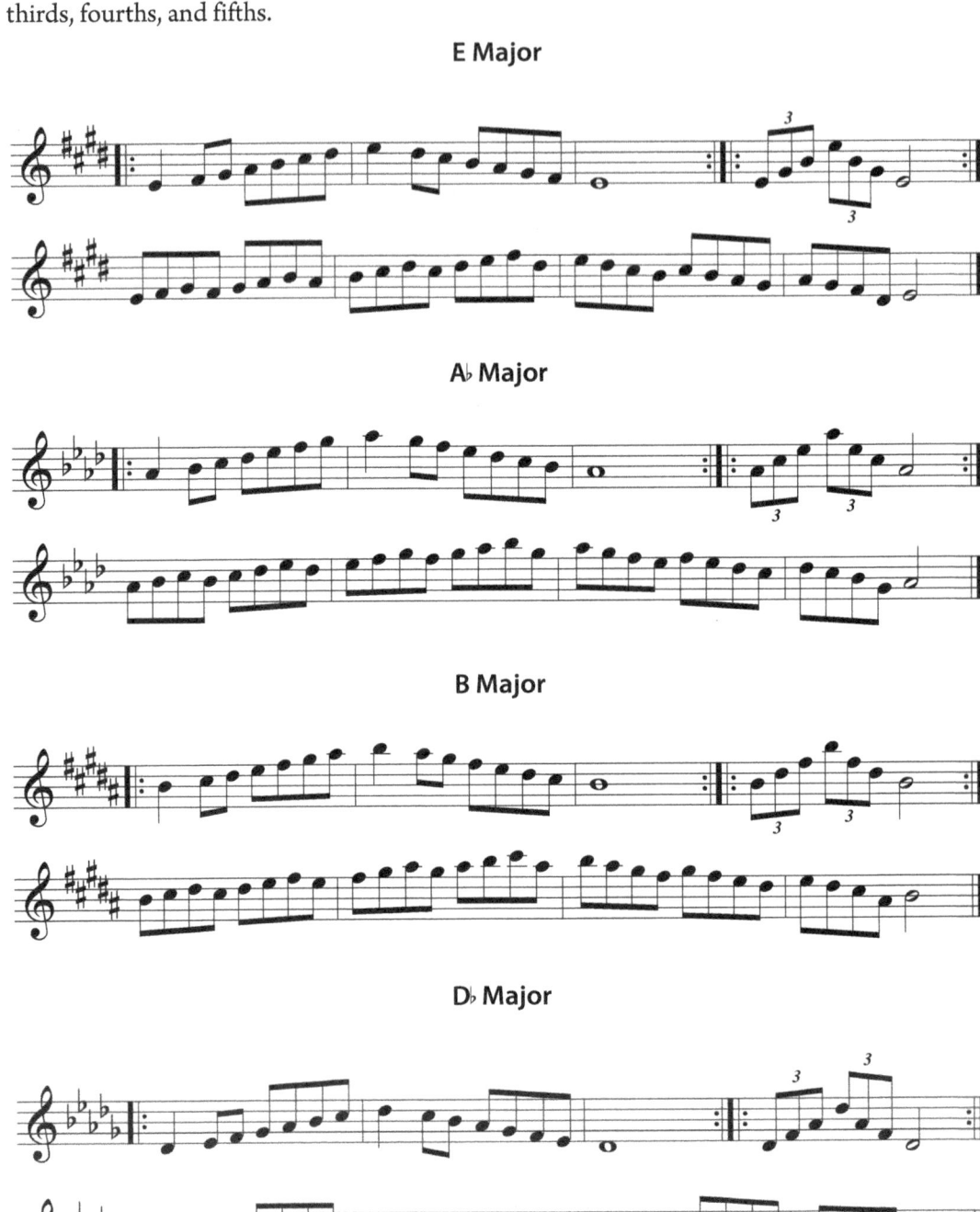

E Major

A♭ Major

B Major

D♭ Major

F♯ Major

G♭ Major

C♯ Major

C♭ Major

Chromatic Scale

Four-Mallet Playing

How to hold two mallets in one hand:

1. Place mallet between middle and ring fingers. Close ring finger and pinky around the shaft of the mallet, and rest middle and index finger on top of mallet.
2. Place other mallet on top of index finger by knuckle, and place thumb on top of mallet.
3. Turn wrist so that the nail of your thumb faces upward.
4. Repeat the process in your other hand.

Mallets are numbered from left to right: 1, 2, 3, 4.

Practice playing quarter notes with each mallet until you feel comfortable with executing the correct technique.

Video 3.3: Four Mallet Grip ▶

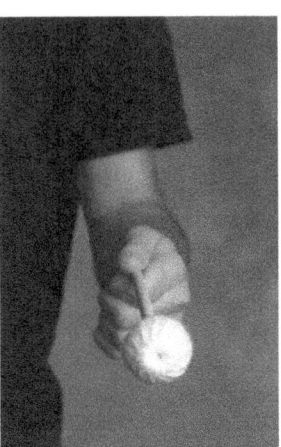
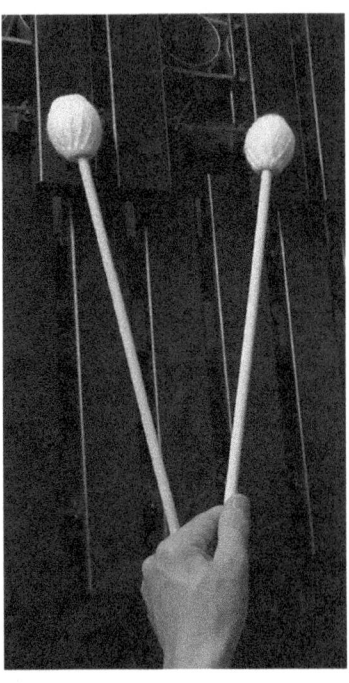

Marimba and the Grand Staff

Practice this exercise with your right hand using mallets 3 and 4. Do the same exercise with mallets 1 and 2.

Now practice all four mallets together.

The following is an exercise in block motion. Keep the shape of the C chord as you progress up the five-note C major scale.

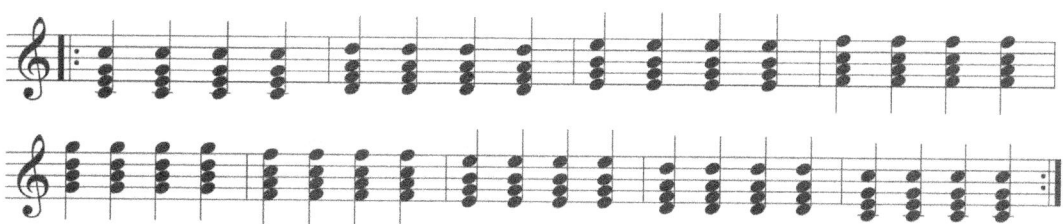

Further Independent Exercises
Practice these exercises with both hands separately.

Grand Staff Exercises

Sunset

for solo marimba

Moderato

Colaneri

Percussionist Spotlight: Mallet Players

Keiko Abe

1937–

Keiko Abe is by far the most renowned virtuosic Japanese marimbist. She started performing professionally at age 13 and went on to study at the Tokyo Gakugei University. She worked in recording studios throughout Japan, performing folk music that she arranged as well as popular music. Her compositions "Dream of the Cherry Blossoms," "Michi," and "Variations on Japanese Children's Songs" have become standard repertoire in universities throughout the world. Abe continues to tour, lecture, and develop instruments for the Yamaha Corporation.

Leigh Howard Stevens

1953–

Born in Orange, New Jersey, Stevens is best known for developing the four-mallet grip that has come to be known as the Stevens Grip. This grip allows for independence with each mallet and is used mostly in playing classical music on the marimba. Stevens started out as a drum set player and then gravitated to the marimba after seeing how quickly he excelled at the instrument while he was at Eastman School of Music. Stevens is known for his interpretation of Bach and other classical music on marimba. In these works, he was able to display his famous technique, the one-handed roll. *Method of Movement for Marimba* is his acclaimed method book for four mallets, and he also runs several companies including Marimba Productions Inc. and Malletech LLC, where he designs cutting-edge mallets and keyboard percussion instruments of the highest quality. He was even on the cover of *Time* magazine! How many percussionists can say that?

Gary Burton

1943–

Born in Indiana, Gary Burton is known as one of the most influential contemporary jazz vibraphone players. His four-mallet grip revolutionized the way people play jazz vibes, giving it a pianistic quality of harmonically playing chords while playing the melody and soloing at the same time. As a high school student, Burton studied vibraphone, marimba, and piano and was highly influenced by pianist Bill Evans. After high school, he attended the Burklee College of Music in Boston. In time he became the president of that college. Gary Burton has played with some of the most noted jazz musicians in history, including Pat Matheney, Gato Barbieri, John Scofield, Keith Jarrett, Chick Corea, Makoto Ozone, Stan Getz, Herbie Hancock, B. B. King, Steve Swallow, and Peter Erskine. Some of his most noted recordings are with Chick Corea in a duo setting. To date, he has been nominated for 21 Grammys and has won 7.

Lionel Hampton

1908–2002

Born in Kentucky, Lionel Hampton was among the first people to play the vibraphone. As a teenager, Hampton took xylophone lessons and started playing drums. His first gigs were playing drums in a Dixieland band and on recording sessions. Around 1927, he started to play a new instrument called the vibraharp. When Louis Armstrong heard him, he asked him to record with him, which propelled Hampton's career as a vibraphonist. As Lionel Hampton rose in popularity, he also raised the visibility of the vibraphone and influenced many future vibraphone players. He went on to play in the Benny Goodman Orchestra and eventually formed his own big band. His most noted songs were "Flying Home" and "Air Mail Special." Hampton, aside from being an amazing musician, was known for his electric showmanship, twirling and flipping his sticks and mallets while playing drums and vibraphone.

Reading Bass Clef

5 Lines   4 Spaces   Expanded Range

G   B   D   F   A   A   C   E   G   D   E   F   B

Sizes of Timpani and Range

23"   26"

29"   32"

Grip

a. French: Thumbs up.

b. German: Palms face down.

c. American: Like German grip but rotate wrists slightly up.

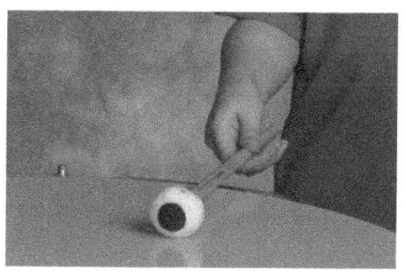 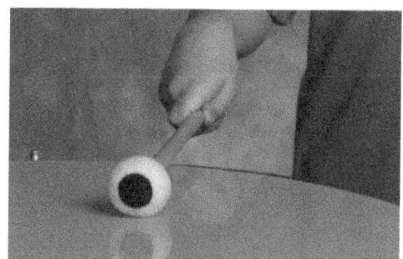 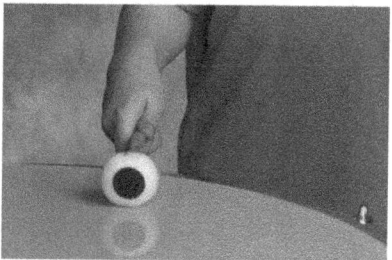

I recommend the French grip. When executed with a fluid wrist lift after the stroke, it brings out the full tone of the timpani.

Beating Spots

For best tone, strike mallets approximately one inch from rim and between the two lugs on each side of the pedal.

     Video 4.1: Grip and Beating Spots ▶

Rolling

When rolling on timpani, use only single-stroke rolls, no double or multiple bounce. The smaller the drum, the faster the roll, and the bigger the drum, the slower the roll.

Placing a Note on the Drum

Pedal up to match the pitch of a mallet instrument. Sing the note into the drum. If the pitch bounces back or sings back to you, the drum is in tune. On most timpani, to raise the pitch, press the pedal forward, and to lower the pitch, add pressure to the pedal from your heel. As you improve your ear training you will be able to tune the timpani using a tuning fork.

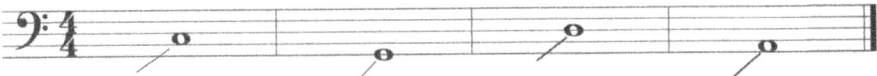

Interval Tuning

Be sure to take the time to get the correct pitches on the drums. Ask your teacher for tips on how to hear and place intervals on the timpani.

Hint: To place a fourth between drums, sing "Here Comes the Bride."

To place a fifth between two drums, sing "Star Wars."

Sticking: The stickings I provide are just recommendations and what feels right to me. Feel free to experiment with making up your own stickings.

One-Drum Tuning Exercises

Muffling

When muffling, use your last three fingers to gently press on the head of the drum to stop the sound. This must be executed very quietly. The general rule is to muffle on the rests.

R: Right hand; L: Left hand; M: Muffle.

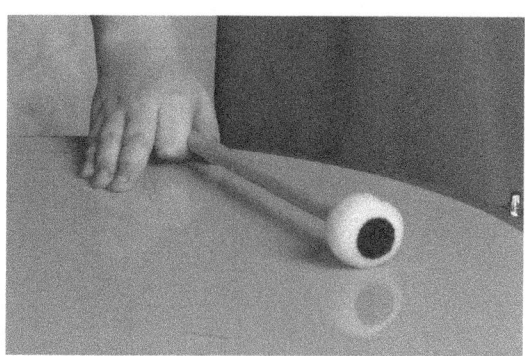

R MR L ML   R MR L ML   R   LMR   RML   LMR

Crossovers

Crossovers allow the player to alternate sticking from one drum to another without having to repeat the same sticking. They allow for a smooth transition and balance in volume.

X=Crossover

Crossovers

Video 4.2: Muffling and Crossovers ▶

Two-Drum Timpani Etudes

I

Follow the Leader

Track 4.1 ▶

C–G

Muffle on rests.

Bartók

II

Symphony #1

Track 4.2 ▶

C–G

Brahms

III

Melody

Track 4.3 ▶

C–G

Schumann

IV

Rebound

Track 4.4 ▶

C–G

Colaneri

V

Toreador

Track 4.5

D-A

Bizet

VI

Hungarian Folk Song

Track 4.6

D-A

Bartók

VII

Bacchanale

Track 4.7 ▶

D-A

Saint-Saëns

Timpani Solos

Two-Drum Unaccompanied

I

II

III

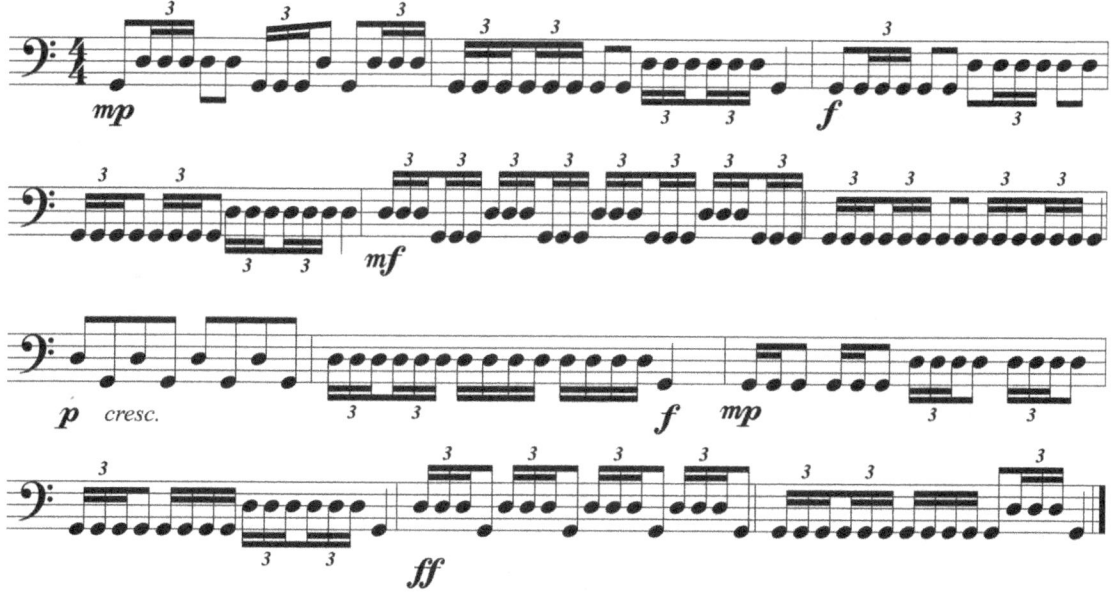

IV

V

VI

VII

Four-Drum Unaccompanied

Timpani Solo

Percussionist Spotlight: Timpanists

Everett "Vic" Firth

1930–

Born in Winchester, Massachusetts, Vic Firth is most known for his stick and mallet company, the Vic Firth Corporation. In his formative years, Firth studied various band instruments and ultimately found his way as a percussionist. In high school, he even led his own big band. Firth went on to attend the New England Conservatory of Music and also to study timpani with Saul Goodman, who was teaching at Julliard at the time. The highlight of Firth's career is his 50-year tenure as timpanist with the Boston Symphony Orchestra. He performed under the great batons of Leonard Bernstein, Leopold Stokowski, and Vladimir Horowitz. Firth is also known for his timpani and snare drum etudes, which are performed by many university percussion students throughout the world.

Saul Goodman

1907–1996

Born in Brooklyn, New York, Saul Goodman is known as the one of the greatest timpanists of all time. His most noted work is his 46 years with the New York Philharmonic. He also taught at the Julliard School of Music for 41 years. Some of his students who went on to illustrious careers were Vic Firth, Bill Kraft, and Gerry Carlyss. Many do not know that he also taught several great jazz drummers of his day, including Gene Krupa, Louie Bellson, and Cozy Cole. Goodman is also known for inventing the chain-driven timpani and replaceable-ball timpani stick. His collections of exercises he used in his lessons were compiled to become the acclaimed timpani method book, *Modern Method for Tympani*, which has become the standard in timpani pedagogy.

Traps

Here we will be covering the traps techniques that percussionists are expected to know in order to perform in the concert band and percussion ensemble settings.

For a further in-depth explanation on how to execute these techniques, refer to our website.

Instruments covered are:

Tambourine
Triangle
Crash Cymbals
Bass Drum
And more!

Tambourine

The Basic Rock Tambourine Pattern: These rhythms can be used to accompany any rock feel.

For some students, this technique comes naturally, but for some it can take a while to get used to this motion.

To start:

1. Hold the tambourine in your dominant hand.
2. Bend your elbow to a 45-degree angle.
3. Swing your hand inward toward the center of your chest by bending your wrist and striking your nondominant hand.
4. Swing your hand outward back to the starting position.

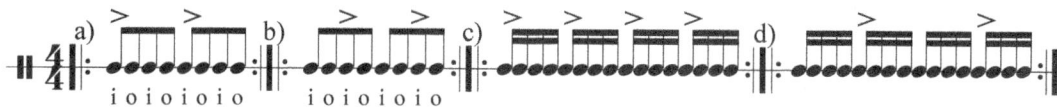

In exercises b, c, d, and e, the accents signify to hit the tambourine on the palm of your nondominant hand.

The Shake Roll Exercise: To execute the shake roll,

1. Hold tambourine in your dominant hand.
2. Rotate your wrist as if you are turning a doorknob (right to left).

3. Start out slowly and gradually speed up.
4. Remember to stay loose and relaxed.
5. This technique should eventually be learned using both hands.

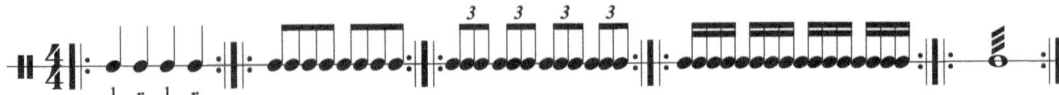

The Measured Shake Roll: Concert playing position.

Hold the tambourine at a 45-degree angle, and strike with your dominant hand.

To execute a measured shake roll, stop the roll on the quarter note by striking the tambourine against the palm of your nondominant hand.

Dynamics

Forte: Strike with your fist on the head of the tambourine.

Mezzo Piano and Mezzo Forte: Strike slightly off-center, with all fingertips touching each other.

Piano: Strike tambourine over the jingles lightly, with fingertips touching each other.

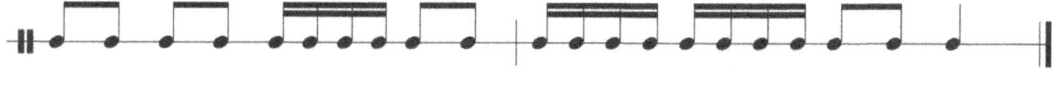

Knee Fist: The knee fist technique is a great technique to use when you are playing fast and loud passages.

1. Place your dominant foot on a small stool.
2. Hold the tambourine in your dominant hand, and have the head face your knee.
3. Place your nondominant hand above the tambourine, making a fist.
4. Strike the tambourine between your nondominant hand and knee.

    k = knee; f = fist.

Dynamics and Rolls

When playing a crescendo roll, hold the tambourine at your side, and raise it in the air as you intensify the roll. When playing the decrescendo roll, hold the tambourine at eye level and gradually lower the tambourine down to your side, decreasing shake intensity.

    For rolling piano on a tambourine, you can implement the thumb roll. Gently rub your thumb around the circumference of the tambourine over the jingles. This vibrates the head and causes the jingles to shake. Have your teacher show you how to apply beeswax to the head to create the necessary friction for executing this technique.

    Video 5.1: Tambourine Technique ▶

Putting It All Together

Surprise

Track 5.1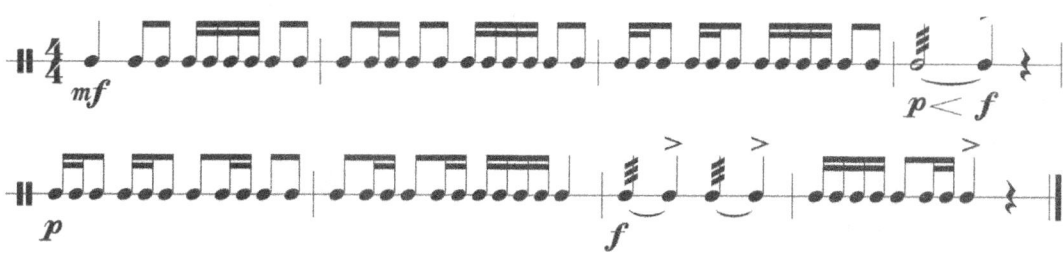

Haydn

On Wings of Song

Track 5.2

Mendelssohn

Evening in the Meadow

Track 5.3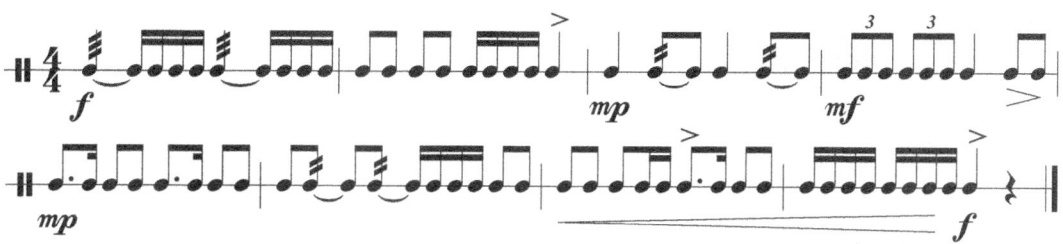

Rebikoff

Triangle

Holding: Form a C shape with your nondominant hand, and place the triangle clip, wide end facing you, on your thumb and middle finger. Rest your index finger on top of the clip. Hold the triangle at eye level, with the opening facing out toward your nondominant side.

 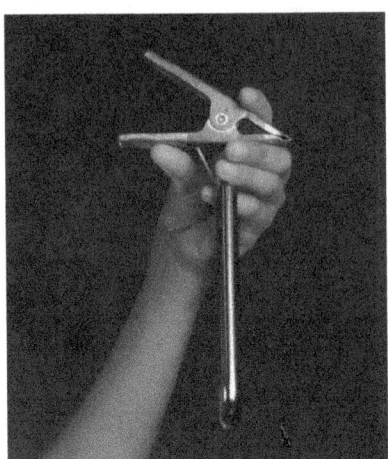

Striking: For nonrolled strokes, strike the triangle on the bottom leg in the center, holding the beater in your dominant hand. Please never use a drumstick to play the triangle.

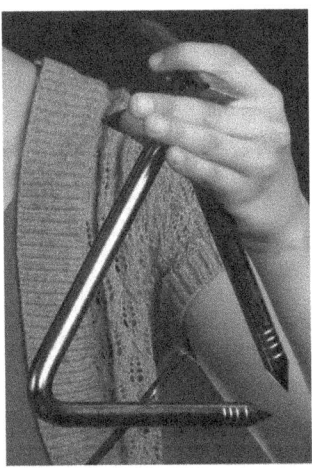

Rolling: Strike the triangle in the corner opposite the opening. For forte, use long strokes; for piano, use fast, short strokes.

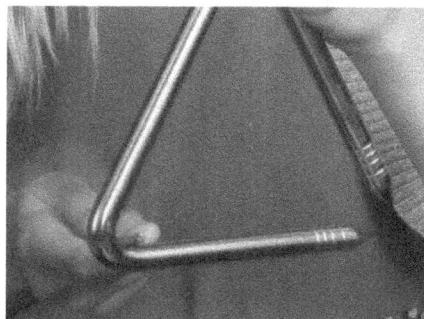

Muffling: Use last three fingers on your nondominant hand, and grip the left leg of the triangle to mute the sound.

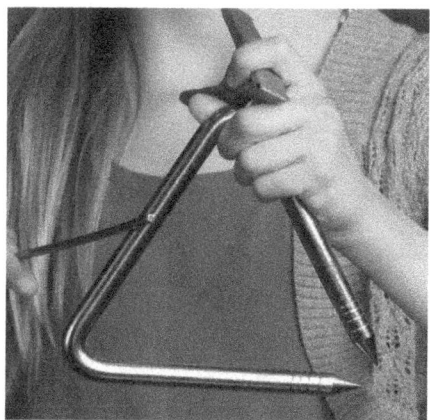

Video 5.2: Triangle Technique ▶

Dynamics

Muffling

a)

b)

c)

d)

(Muffle on rests above staff to the left)

Rolls

To a Wild Rose

Track 5.4 ▶

MacDowell

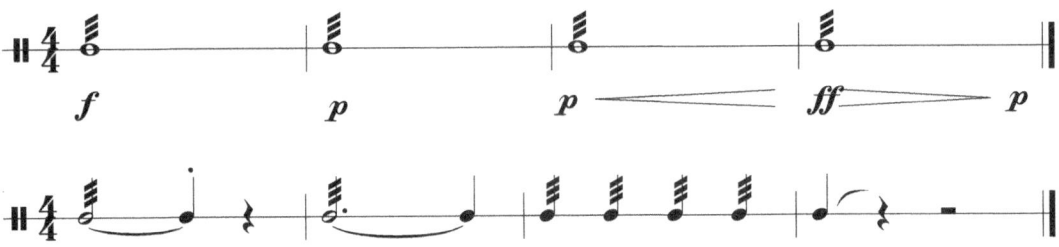

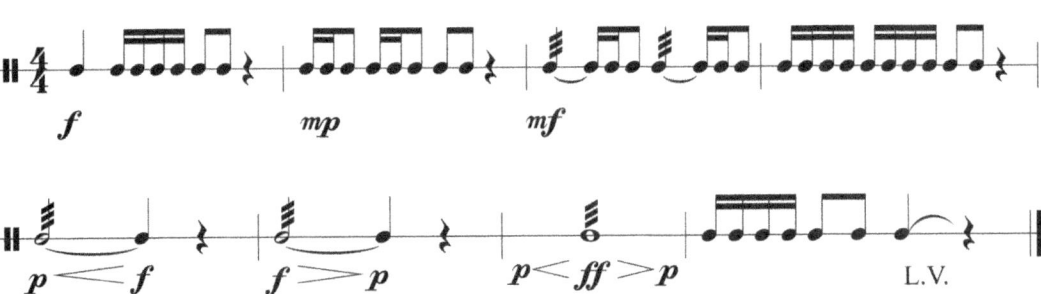

Crash Cymbals

Holding: Wrap your hand around the cymbal strap with your thumb on top. The rest of the fingers grip the strap into the palm. Do not put your hands through the loops. Hold the cymbals at a 45-degree angle with each plate about two to three inches apart, depending on the dynamic you are playing.

Striking: There are two approaches to playing crash cymbals:

a. Top of the upper cymbal strikes the top of the lower cymbal and swiftly slides up.
b. Bottom of the top cymbal strikes the bottom of the lower cymbal, and then the upper parts of both cymbals strike together. When played fast, this creates a flam type of motion.

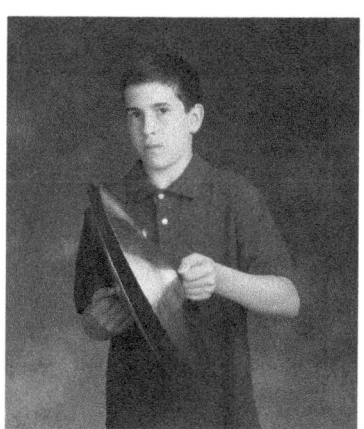 

Dampening: To stop the sound, pull the cymbals into your chest.

Video 5.3: Crash Cymbal Technique ▶

Dynamics: When playing piano, keep the cymbals close together; when playing forte, start the strike from farther away.

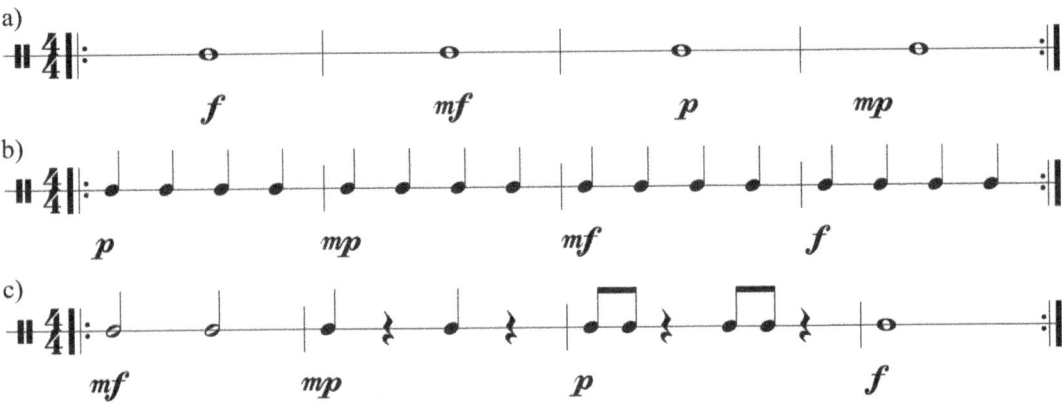

Petra

Track 5.5 ▶

Colaneri

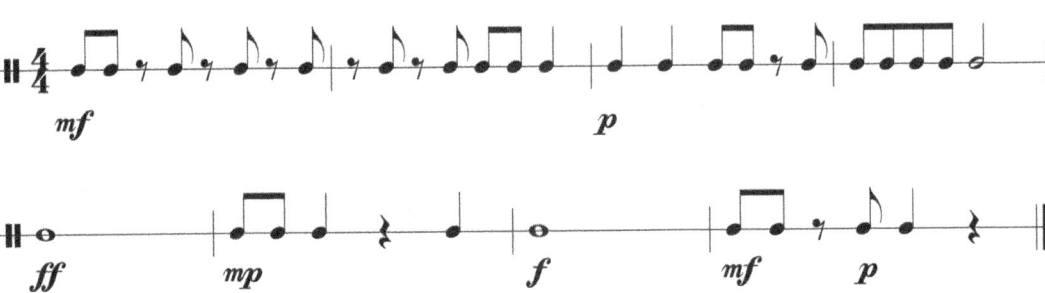

Bass Drum

Striking: Hold beater in your right hand, and strike the bass drum slightly off-center. Beater should flow in a continuous elliptical motion from bottom to top. For louder strokes, use your forearm and wrist. Softer strokes should be played using just your wrist.

Muffling: Your left hand should reach around to the other side of the bass drum and slightly dampen it with your fingers and/or full hand. Your right foot should rest on a stool. Use your right knee to press against the head for dampening.

Rolls: Use two beaters and roll on the right side of head approximately two to three inches from the rim, depending on the size of the drum. Use single strokes. If the bass drum has a tilting system, you can set it to a 45-degree angle.

Video 5.4: Bass Drum Technique ▶

Bass Drum Exercises and Etude

Pavane

Track 5.6 ▶

Fauré

More Trap Instruments

Suspended Cymbals

Beating Spots: Edge (rim), bow (surface), and bell (dome).

Mallets: Yarn or stick. Do not use timpani mallets.

Practice exercise by experimenting with an assortment of mallets and beating spots.

Temple Blocks

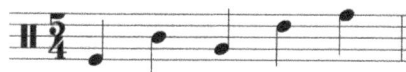

Usually come with five blocks that are notated using the five lines of the staff.

Mallets: Rubber mallets. Do not use timpani mallets.

Castanets

Mounted: Played with hands and sits on a trap table or sturdy music stand with a towel on it.

Handheld: Can be played in the air or stuck against your leg.

Tam-tam

Always prep the tam-tam before striking by tapping your fingers lightly on the surface to initiate vibration. Then, strike the tam-tam slightly off-center. To roll, start on the outside and work your way in.

Most people confuse a tam-tam for a gong. A gong is a pitched instrument, and a tam-tam has an indefinite pitch.

Percussionist Spotlight: Classical Percussionists

Neil Grover

1955–

Raised in Bellmore, New York, Neil Grover attended the New England Conservatory of Music and went on to perform with the Boston Pops, Boston Symphony, American Ballet Theater, and many other world-renowned ensembles. He recorded for the rock group Aerosmith, performed in Broadway's *Pirates of Penzance*, and recorded percussion tracks for the movie *Indiana Jones and the Temple of Doom*. Grover has held posts as percussion professor at Boston Conservatory and the University of Massachusetts. He has given clinics all around the country and is the CEO and founder of Grover Pro Percussion, which is known around the world for its high-quality triangles and tambourines.

Alan Abel

1930–

Born in Hobart, Indiana, Alan Abel received his formal training from the Eastman School of Music. While there, he performed with the Rochester Philharmonic and then went on to play with the US Air Force Band. Abel next took the principal percussion chair with the Oklahoma City Symphony. After a six-year stint in Oklahoma, he went on to a 38-year career with the Philadelphia Orchestra as associate principal percussionist. Abel has served on faculty at Rutgers University, Rowan University, Temple University, and several other universities throughout the country. He has several method books out and is known around the world for his conception of the Alan Able Triangle.

In this chapter, there are some basic to intermediate rock, jazz, and world drum-set beats to get you started. Once you have mastered these beats, I encourage you to make up your own and write them out. There are also some basic fills to get you started, and I encourage you to experiment with creating your own fills. You can use exercises from the sticking and accent portion of this book and experiment with placing the notes onto different toms around the set. You can also take portions of the snare drum exercises to use as fills.

The key to understanding how to read drum-set music is to think more vertical than horizontal. It's all about lining up the snare, bass, and hi-hat. Speed is not as important as developing the coordination. As they say, slow and steady wins the race.

Technique

Holding the sticks for a drum set is similar to playing the snare drum, but your thumbs can turn up a little by slightly rotating your wrist out.

Posture

Posture is often overlooked in talking about the drum set. Drummers who do not develop good posture end up having back problems in the future. Often drummers slouch when they play, which leads to putting extra pressure on the lower back. So make sure you sit up straight when playing.

Dominant hand crossover: The dominant hand crosses over the nondominant hand to play the hi-hat, and the nondominant hand plays the snare drum. This technique is used so that the hi-hat, which plays the most notes, is played by the strongest hand.

Bass Drum

For playing rock beats, it has become standard to play with heel up. Your toe should be about half an inch away from the top of the pedal, and the heel should be slightly raised. Try to get a good rebound off the head of the bass drum so it makes a full tone.

For playing jazz, it is standard to play with the heel down and less rebound off the bass drumhead. In both styles, you do not want the beater to stick to the head after impact.

 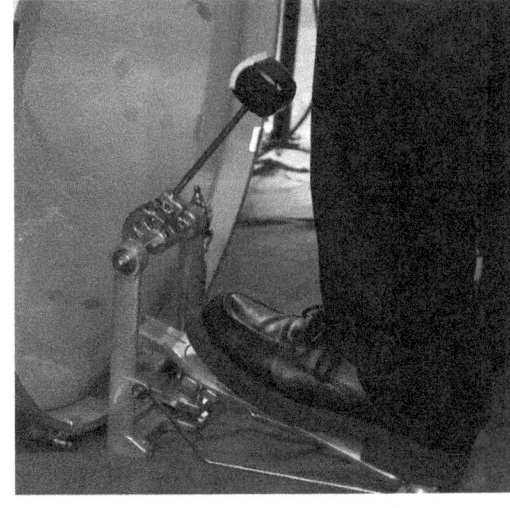

Hi-Hat

I always start students playing the rock beat using eighth notes on the hi-hat. I usually clamp the hi-hat shut so that students do not have to concern themselves with keeping pressure on the pedal. The hi-hat should be positioned so that the edge of the hi-hat hangs above or slightly away from the snare drum rim. Your dominant hand strikes the hi-hat with the top part of the shaft of the stick.

Snare Drum

Keep the snare drum straight so that you can comfortably hit a rimshot when needed. Some players do have a slight inward tilt. Do not keep the snare height at your knees. It has to be high enough so when you bend your elbows to play, they bend a little over a 90-degree angle, and the sticks rest comfortably on the snare head.

Mounted Toms

Place toms close to the snare drum, with a small tilt inward toward the snare.

Floor Tom

A floor tom should be a bit lower than the snare drum.

Ride Cymbal

The ride cymbal should hang a little over the floor tom and second tom.

Crash Cymbal

The crash cymbal can be on right and/or left side. Keep the crash cymbals hanging tilted inward slightly over the toms.

Parts of the Drum Set

A. Snare Drum

B. Bass Drum

C. Mounted Tom 1

D. Mounted Tom 2

E. Floor Tom

F. Hi-Hat

G. Ride Cymbal

H. Crash Cymbal

Video 6.1: Drum Set Basics

Rock Drumming

Drum-set key

The basic rock beat

Track 6.1

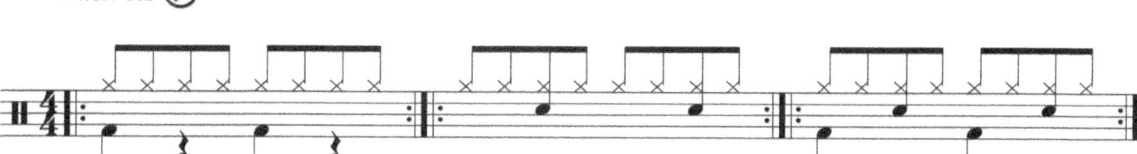

The basic rock fill

Track 6.2

Beat with fill

Track 6.3

Variation

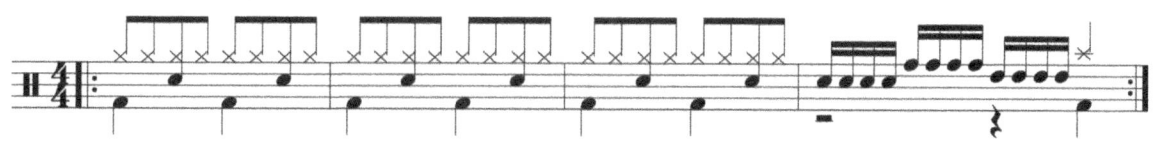

Crash on one

Track 6.4

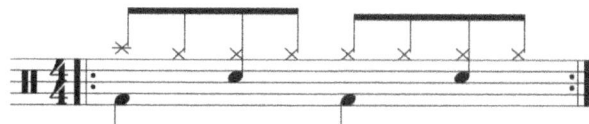

Putting it all together

Track 6.5 ▶
Crash on repeat only

Fill With Bass Drum

Beat and Fill With Bass Drum

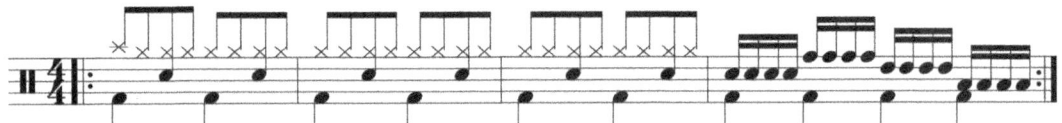

Beat With Four on the Floor

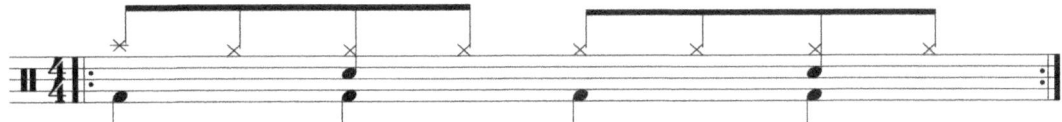

Beat and Fill With Four on the Floor

More Beats

Track 6.6

Mixing it up

Beats, Beats, and More Beats

Track 6.7 ▶

More Fill Ideas

Combining Beats and Fills

Track 6.8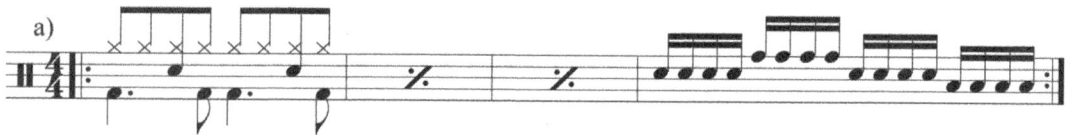

a)

b)

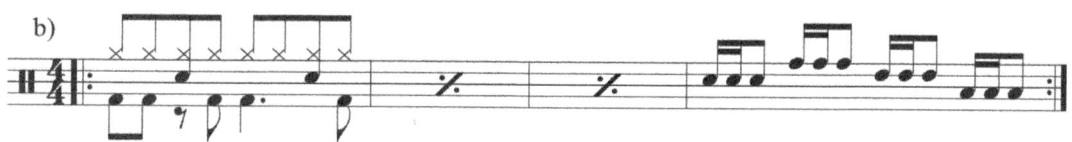

c)

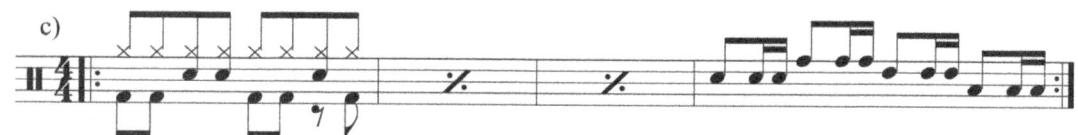

d)

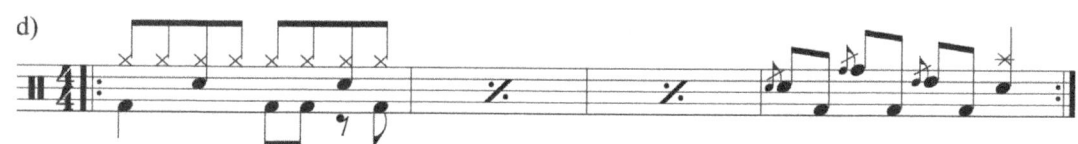

e)

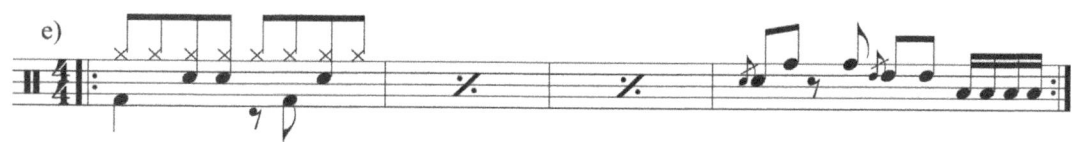

f)

16th-Note Combinations between Hands and Feet

These grooves should be played slowly at first. Once you have mastered them, feel free to add accents to enhance the feel. Ultimately, the coordination developed from these exercises will lead to developing your own grooves. I encourage you to improvise from these rhythms and consider changing the playing surfaces.

Track 6.9

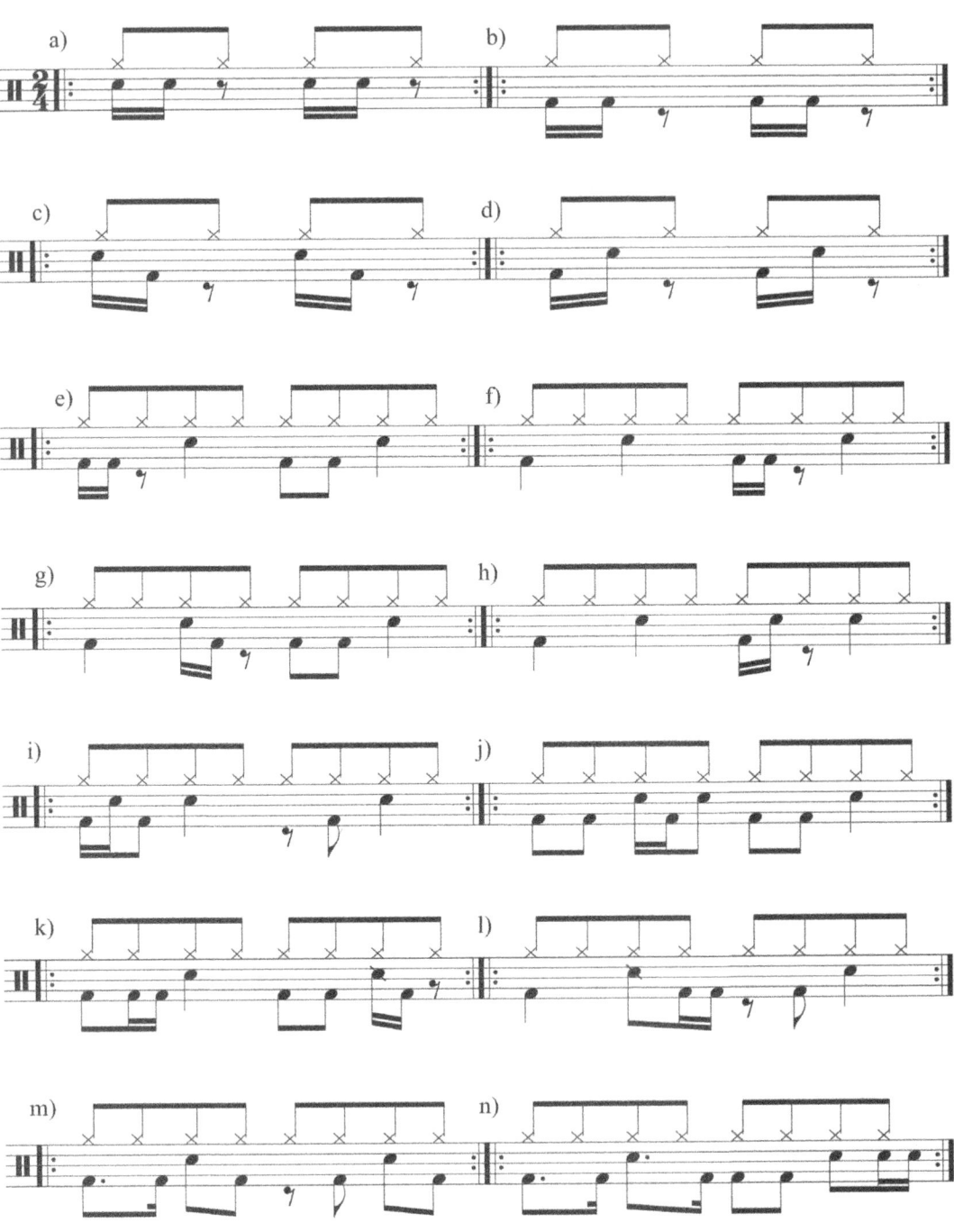

Track 6.10 ▶

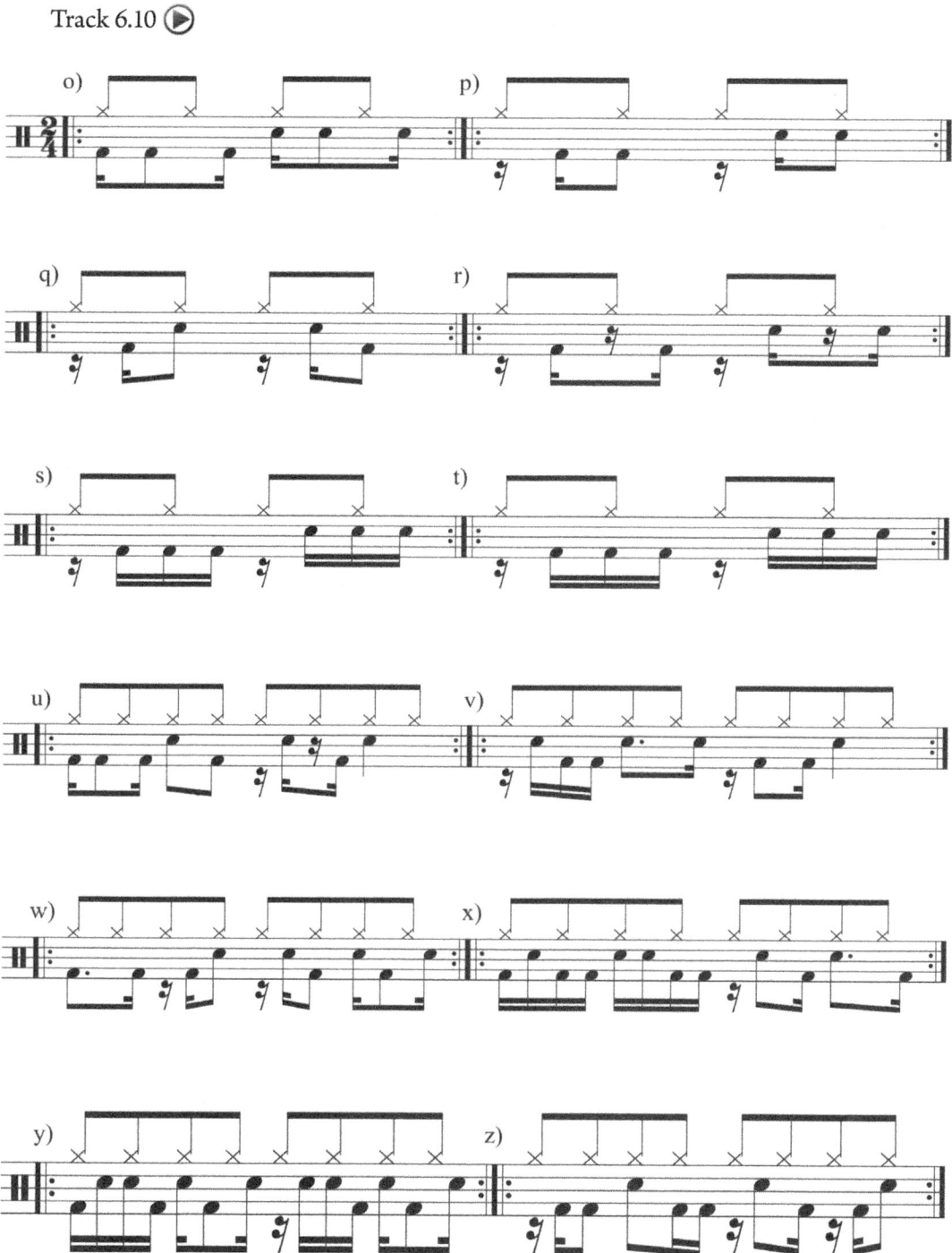

Disco/club beats

Track 6.11 ▶

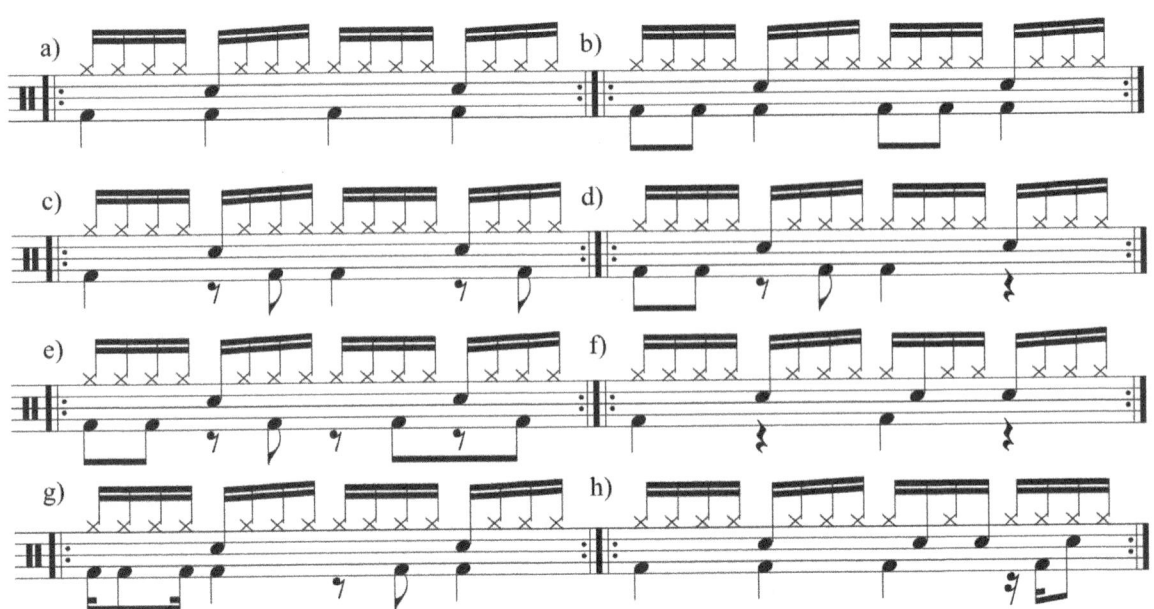

Shuffles

Track 6.12 ▶

Jazz Drumming

Building the swing beat

Track 6.13 ▶

Play on ride cymbal

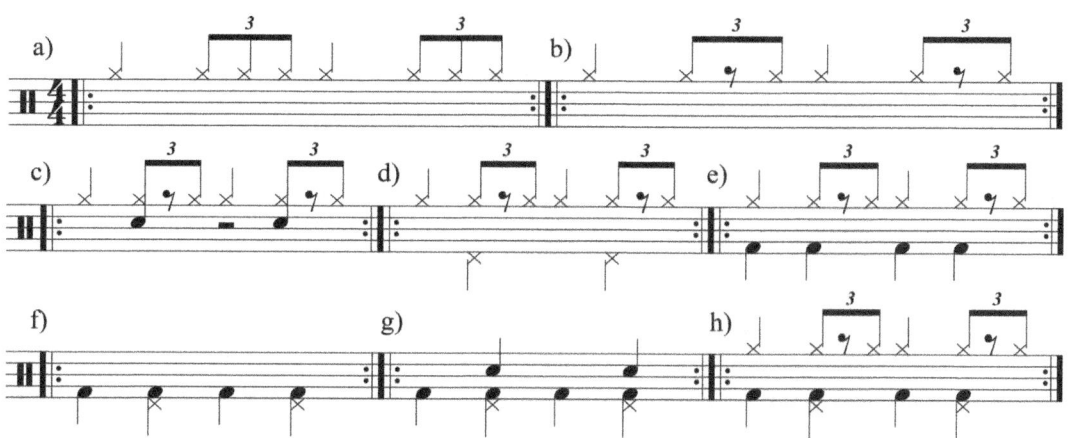

The swing beat with foot-on-the-floor

Track 6.14 ▶

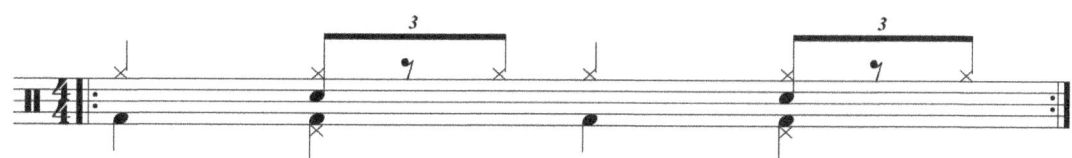

Two beat

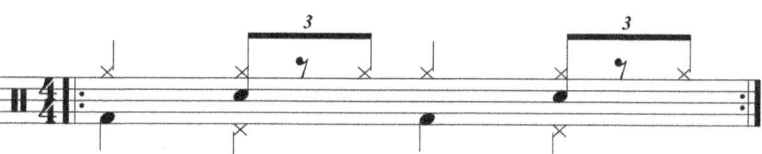

Swinging on the hi-hat

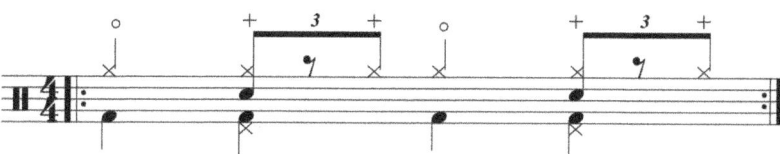

Variation

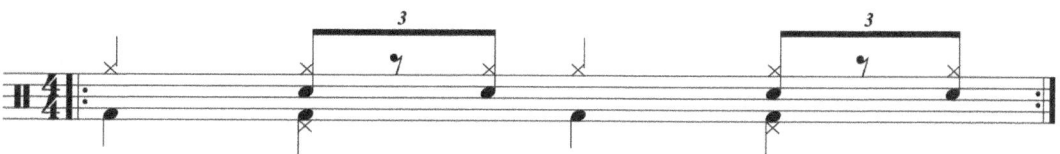

Basic jazz fill

More jazz fills

Coming out of a fill

Crash on one

Putting it all together

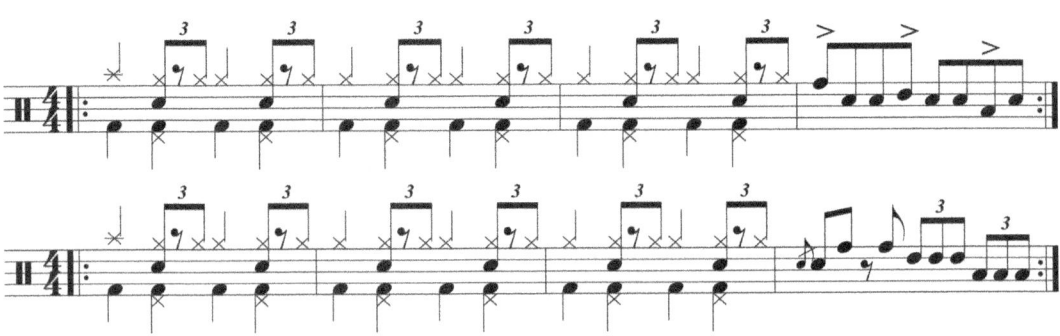

Swing Beat Independence

Track 6.15

Ensemble Figures in the Big Band Setting

Ensemble figures are rhythms displayed above the staff that indicate to the drummer the rhythms that are being played by the brass section. These figures are also referred to as "horn hits."

Column A shows the common way ensemble figures are written in drum charts for jazz bands. Column B shows what the drummer will actually play. Often drummers play fills that lead into an ensemble figure or play a fill within the figure. This concept is called "setting up the ensemble figure." Column C displays how to set up the ensemble figure. A good general rule of thumb is to play notes with a quarter-note value and over on surfaces that sustain like the crash cymbal with the bass drum. Notes of lesser value should be played on a surface with less of a sustain, such as the snare drum or tom. Once you learn the coordination for each exercise, I recommend playing three measures of the swing beat and then playing a measure from column C and continuing to play the swing beat.

Sample Big Band Charts

Swing

Track 6.16 Slow ▶
Track 6.17 Fast ▶

Rock

Track 6.18 Slow ▶
Track 6.19 Fast ▶

Latin

Track 6.20 Slow ▶
Track 6.21 Fast ▶

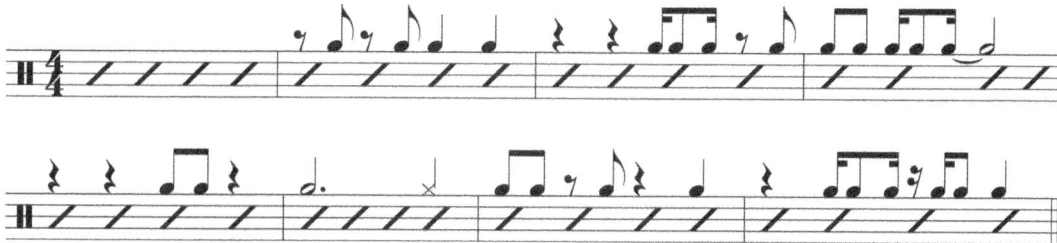

Track 6.22 Slow ▶
Track 6.23 Fast ▶

World Beat Drum Set Grooves

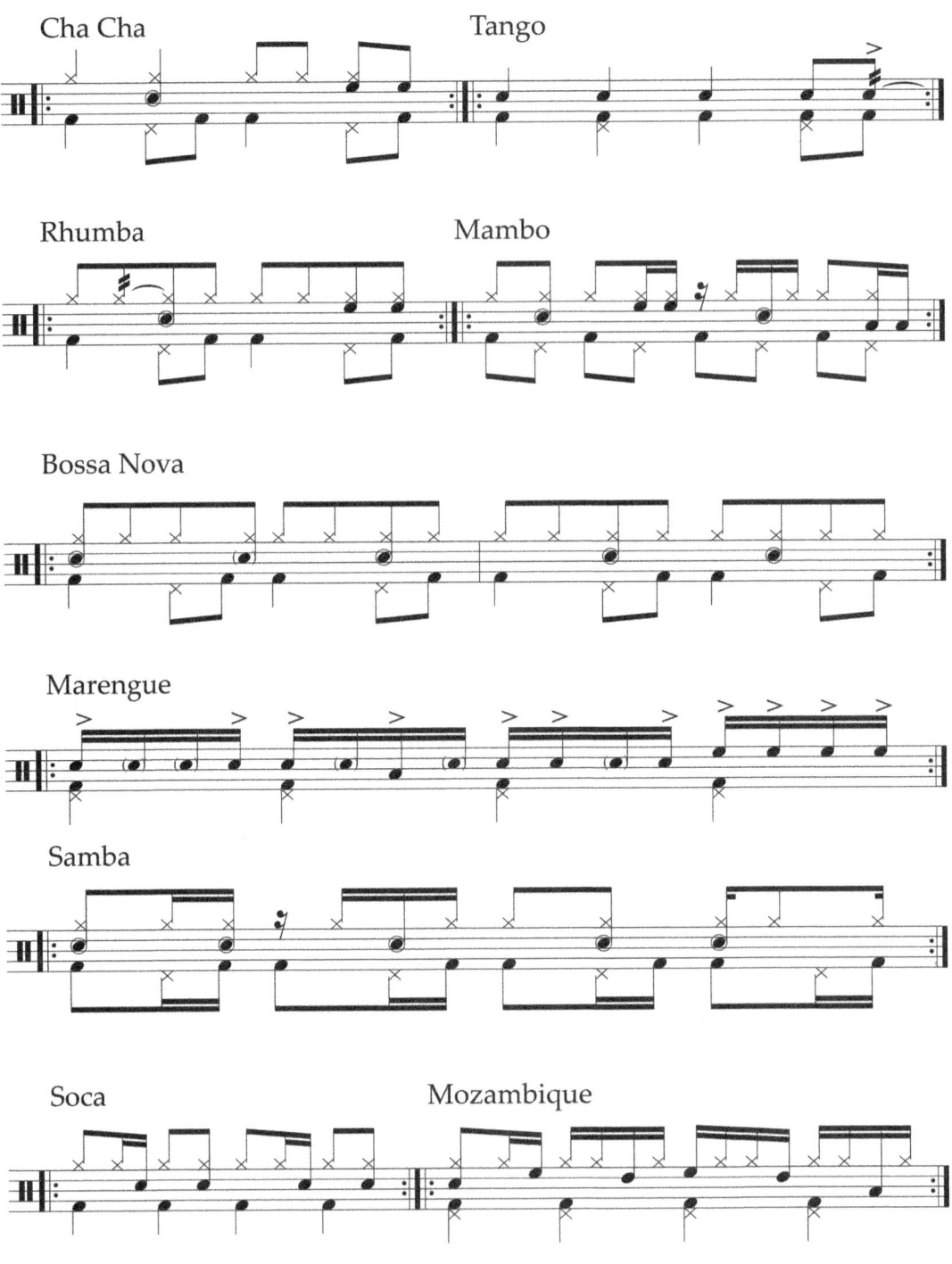

Video 6.2: World Beats for Drum Set ▶

Percussionist Spotlight: Drum Set Players

Buddy Rich

1917–1987

Bernard "Buddy" Rich was born in Manhattan, New York, and has been considered the greatest drummer of all time. He possessed great technique, speed, and groove. He was even known for being able to play a one-handed drum roll. Rich started playing drums as a child in the New York vaudeville scene. He fronted his own big band at age 11 and went on to an illustrious career performing with some of the biggest names of his time, including Frank Sinatra, Artie Shaw, the Andrews Sisters, the Tommy Dorsey Orchestra, and the Muppets, just to name a few.

Neil Peart

1952–

Canadian-born percussionist Neil Peart is best known for his work with the progressive rock group Rush, particularly his amazing technique and intricate fills as he plays through odd time signatures. He also writes the lyrics for the band. Peart's first drum lessons were at age 14, when he studied at the Peninsula Conservatory of Music. Upon graduation, Peart played in local rock bands and was heavily influenced by British rock drummer Keith Moon, as well as by John Bonham. He later found inspiration in the great jazz drummers Buddy Rich and Gene Krupa. Peart played in local Canadian rock bands before leaving for London to make a living as a drummer. After a short stint in England, he returned to Canada to play with another local band before joining Rush in 1974. With the band Rush, Peart recorded 24 gold records and 14 platinum records. The band has toured around the world, and Neil Peart continues to hold many distinguished drum awards from every major drum magazine.

In this chapter, we are going to explore common world percussion instruments and rhythms that are often found in school concert band, jazz band, and percussion ensemble music. This chapter is designed so that once these techniques are learned and these rhythms are mastered, students will be able to combine the rhythms from the different instruments and create their own percussion ensemble arrangements. This can be done in a drum circle format, or they can accompany some of the melodies from the mallet portion of this book.

Drum Circle Ideas

a. Call and Response: One person plays a rhythm, and everyone else plays back the same rhythm.

b. Solos: Everyone stops and one person takes a solo, or everyone lowers volume and the soloist plays over their rhythms.

c. Trade Fours: Everyone stops, and two people take turns soloing for four measures each.

d. Ostinato: Students enter one at a time, playing a repeated pattern.

e. Unison: Everyone plays the same rhythm.

f. Incorporate Dynamics: Make sure to shape the performance with louds and softs.

g. Sequence: Rhythms can get passed around the circle one at a time.

h. Feel free to add singing, chanting, and dancing!

To change into new sections of the drum circle, you need a leader to give visual or rhythmic cues.

Have fun!

Conga

Strokes

open (o): Keep your fingers together and strike the conga with the top part of your palm and fingers. Keep your thumb up. Your stroke should be relaxed and free of tension. After striking the drum, use a lifting motion to bring out the full tone of the drum.

closed (c): Strike the drum in the same manner as the open stroke, but keep your hand on the head of drum to mute the sound.

dead (d): With your fingers together, strike the center of the drum with your palm.

slap (s): Cup your hand and strike the surface with your last three fingers. You can lift or keep your hand on the drum, depending on the desired sound. You can place your other hand on the head and apply pressure to get a sharper pop.

palm/finger (p, f): Drop your palm on the conga head, and then tap your fingers and rock back and forth.

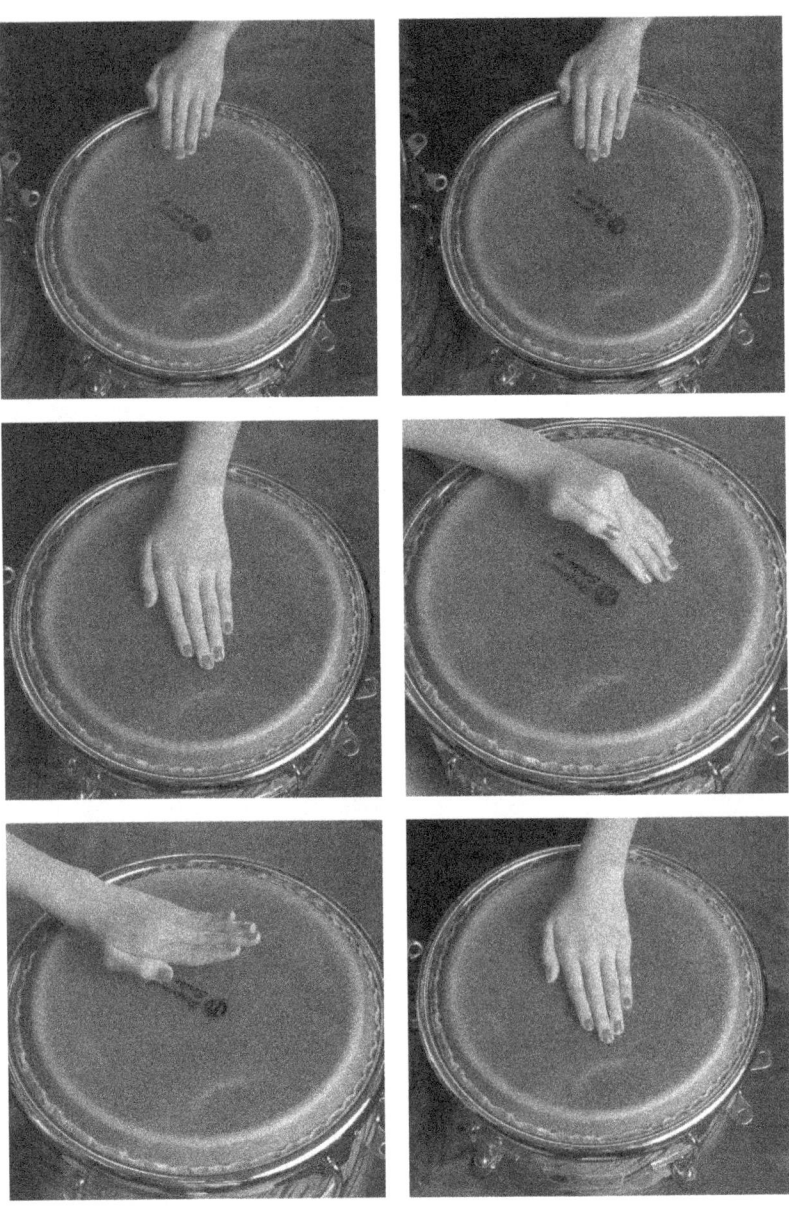

Types of Drums

These types of drums are the requinto (highest drum), quinto (high drum), conga (middle drum), and tumba (low drum). This chapter focuses on the two most commonly used drums, the conga and the tumba. When you are using two drums, the conga drum should be on your nondominant side.

Video 7.1: Congas Technique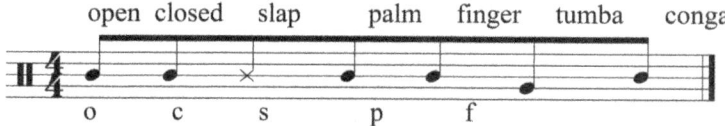

Conga Key:

Track 7.1 can be used as a play-along for all Latin percussion instruments. ▶

One-Drum Warm-ups

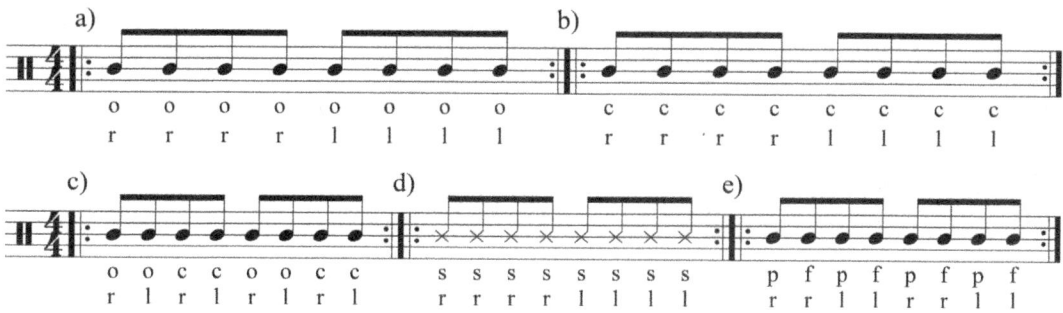

One-Drum Tumbao

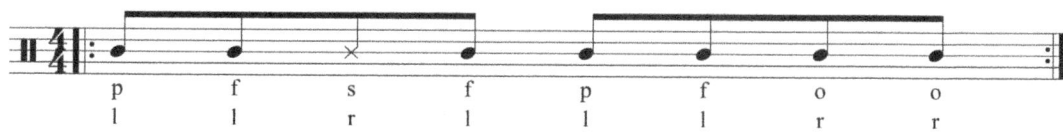

Two-Drum Tumbao

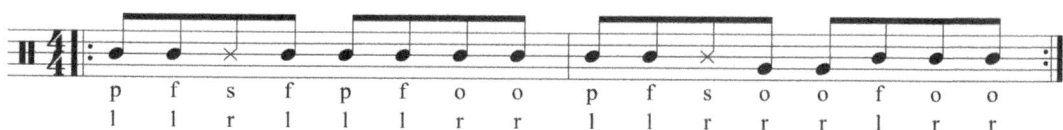

Pop Conga Beat

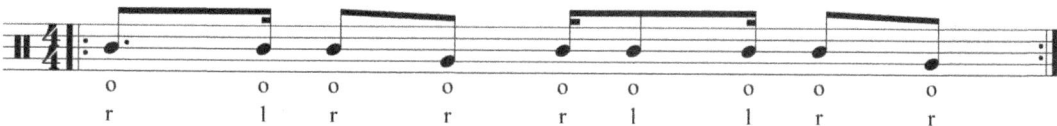

Bongos

Playing position: On a stand or held between legs, with the high drum slightly elevated.

Strokes: Play with fingertips (f) and outside thumb (t). Use a quick lifting motion when striking with your fingers.

Video 7.2: Bongo Technique ▶

Basic Pattern: Martillo

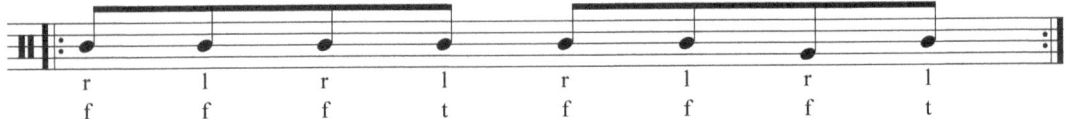

Timbales

Playing Position and Setup: Timbales should be positioned at waist height, with the small drum to your dominant side. They are played with two thin wooden sticks.

Technique: A cowbell may be mounted on the timbales, or you can play rhythms on the shell of your drum. These are called paila rhythms.

Grip: Hold sticks the way you would for drum-set playing. Cross stick—marked with an x—is to be played by clicking the stick in the nondominant hand on the rim while the bottom part of the stick rests on the drumhead.

Often, timbale players use rimshots when soloing.

Video 7.3: Timbale Technique ▶
Timbale Key:

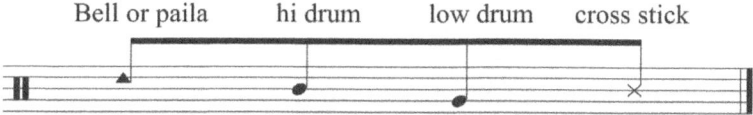

Bell or paila   hi drum   low drum   cross stick

Coordination Exercise

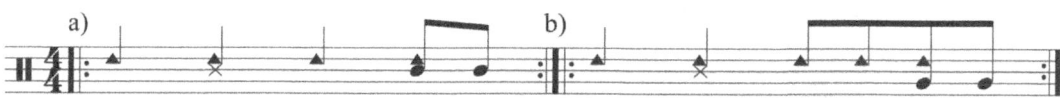

Mambo

Djembe

Holding the drum: Some djembes have feet and only need to be placed in front of the seated performer. Other djembes have an hourglass shape. These djembes can be played standing with a strap or sitting down. When you are playing in a sitting position, the djembe should be placed between your legs and slightly angled away from you.

Babatunde Olatunji, a famous djembe master, coined the following strokes for the djembe back in the 1950s, and they are still used today.

Strokes: The three basic strokes are as follows:

Pronunciation Key: Gun-Guun Dun-Duun,

Go-Go Do-Doo

Pa-Pah Ta-Tah

Bass/Gun (right hand); Dun (left hand): Strike drum center with a lifting motion.

Middle/Go (right hand); Do (left hand): Strike the drum toward edge with the center of the palm and fingers.

High/Pa (right hand); Ta (left hand): Fingers strike the drum from the knuckle to the tip of the fingers.

When executing these strokes, do not use your thumb, and make sure your hands form a triangle between the thumbs and index fingers.

Video 7.4: Djembe Technique ▶

Djembe Key:

Gun/Dun   Go/Do   Pa/Ta

Djembe Drills

Gun Dun . . .   Go Do . . .   Pa Ta . . .

Ibo

Ku Ku

Track 7.2

Fanga

Track 7.3

Player 1

Player 2

Player 3

Break*

*The break is used to transition sections in a drum circle.

More World Percussion Instruments

African

Shikare (shaker): gourd with a net of beads wrapped around it.

Technique: Dominant hand holds gourd by the neck, and the nondominant hand holds it from the bottom. Tilt toward the neck. Shake back and forth away from your chest or back and forth between your hands. You can also strike the bottom of the gourd with your nondominant hand.

Experiment with various accents and rhythms.

Gankogui (agogo bells): Two cowbells connected by a metal curved rod.

Technique: Played with stick.

Djun djun: African bass drum.

There is usually a high drum and a low drum. Strike with a medium-hard mallet.
Technique: Played with rubber-wound mallet.

Brazilian

Sordu: Bass drum, similar to a floor tom.

Technique: Worn with a strap over one shoulder and struck with one mallet; it uses a nondominant-hand dampening technique.

m = muffle; o = open strike, both with mallet.

Caixa: Snare drum.

Technique: Played like a concert snare drum. It is common to play eighth notes in cut time with varied accents and one-hand buzzing.

Tamborim: Like a small tambourine without the jingles.

Technique: Played with a stick or blass stick. Nondominant hand holds instrument, and fingers strike the inside head. x = fingers.

Agogo bells: Two cowbells connected by a metal curved rod.

Technique: Played with stick.

Cuba

Although many of these instruments have different origins, they all migrated to Cuba to make up part of the rhythm section of the dance bands of the 1930s and 1940s.

Clave: Two thick sticks you strike together.

3-2 Clave Rhythm

Technique: Cradle one clave in your nondominant hand so that your fingers are out of the way when the other clave strikes. Be sure to hold the sticks loosely so that the sound is not choked. If you start in the second measure, you have what is called "2-3 clave."

Cowbell: A metal bell with an opening on one side called the mouth.

Technique: Hold the instrument in your nondominant hand with its mouth facing away from your body. Strike the stick on the edge of the center of the mouth. You can also strike with the tip of the stick on the face (flat part).

Low note = mouth; high note = face (flat part).

Guiro: An oblong, hollow, cylindrical wooden or plastic instrument with ridges going across the top and two finger holes for the thumb and index finger.

Technique: Played with a small wooden stick, using a forward and backward scraping motion. The downstroke goes away from the body, the upstroke goes toward the body, and you can also tap the top of the instrument.

d = down; t = tap.

Maracas: Two hollowed-out handheld gourds with beads inside them.

Technique: Held like drumsticks, but the index finger and thumb grip the base of the gourd. They can be played in the air with a snapping motion.

Shaker: Cylindrical tube with beads in it.

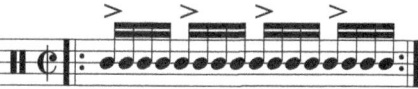

Technique: Shake in and out away from body. Hold at eye level.

Cabasa: Thick wooden cylinder with beads wrapped around it with a handle.

Technique: Hold the instrument in your dominant hand, and use your other hand to hold beads still while your dominant hand rotates the beads back and forth.

Percussionist Spotlight: World Percussionists

Giovanni Hidalgo

1963–

Giovanni Hidalgo is known around the world as a Latin percussionist and conga master. His father and grandfather were both percussionists, and he carried on that tradition. As a performer, he has played with such notable musicians as Dizzy Gillespie, Michel Camilo, Eddie Palmieri, Gloria Estefan, Tito Puente, and Paul Simon, just to name a few. He has several instructional conga videos and has taught at the Berklee College of Music. Giovanni has also received Grammy awards for his work with Mickey Hart and Arturo Sandoval.

Babatunde Olatunji

1927–2003

Nigerian percussionist Babatunde Olatunji is considered the foremost renowned African percussionist in modern times. He was born in the small village of Ajido. He learned traditional African music as a child, but his formal musical education began at age 23, when he came to the United States on a scholarship to study at Morehouse College in Georgia. After graduation, Olatunji studied public administration at New York University. There he started playing percussion gigs, which gave him a connection to Columbia Records. Through this relationship, he brought world music to the masses through his Drums of Passion recordings. Olatunji went on to record with John Coltrane, Carlos Santana, Cannonball Adderley, Horace Silver, Quincy Jones, Stevie Wonder, Max Roach, and Mickey Hart. It was Olatunji who invented the syllable system for teaching djembe, which is used in this book.

Appendix

Bucket Busters

Score

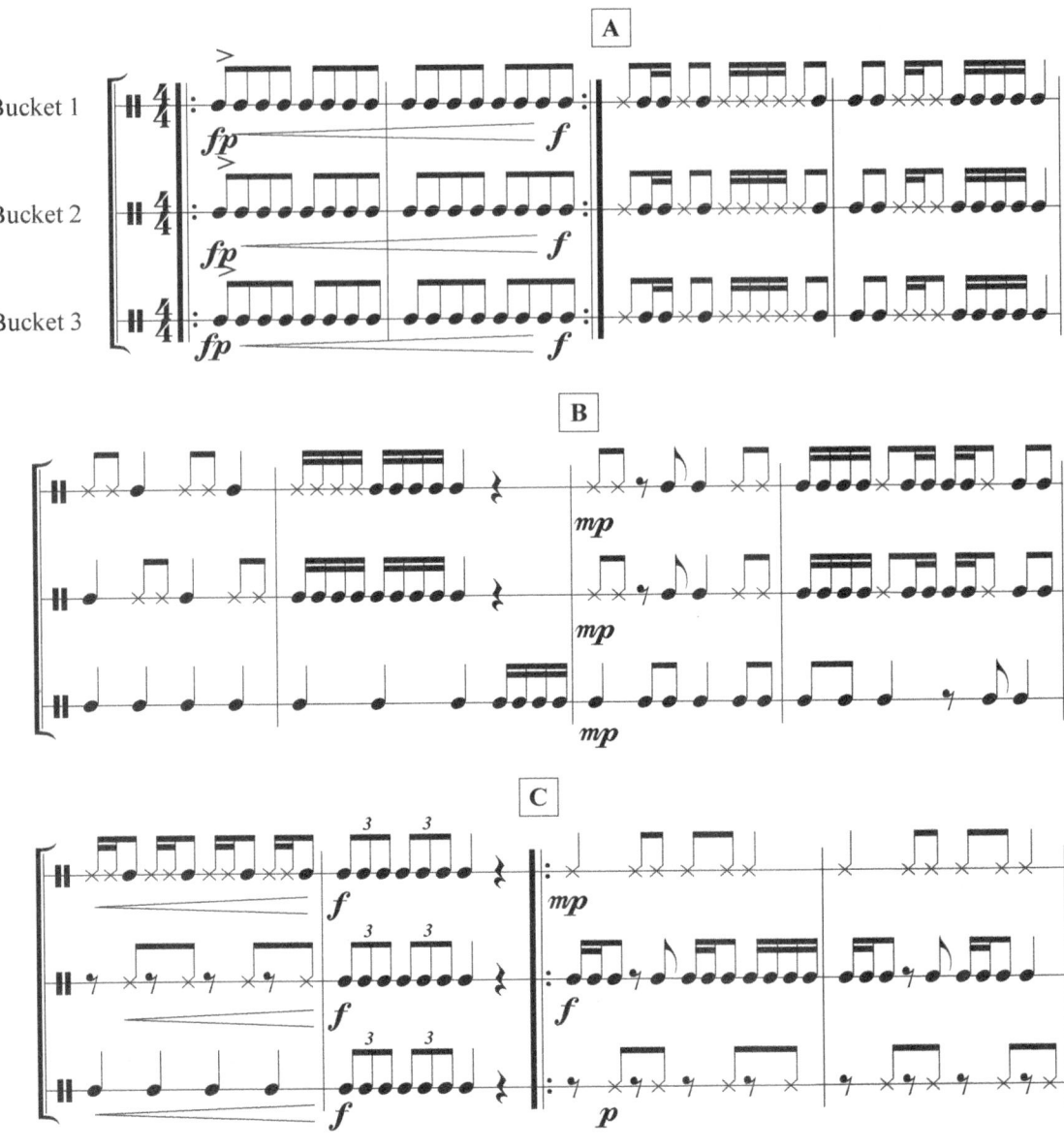

Rim: x

Center: standard notation

Bucket 1 and 2 are to be played on 5-gallon buckets, and Bucket 3 should be played on a 32-gallon bucket. This composition is intended to be played on three buckets. However, you can assign any two surfaces to each player. You can also extend sections and incorporate solos and improvisations using stick clicks and the side of the bucket. As always, have fun!

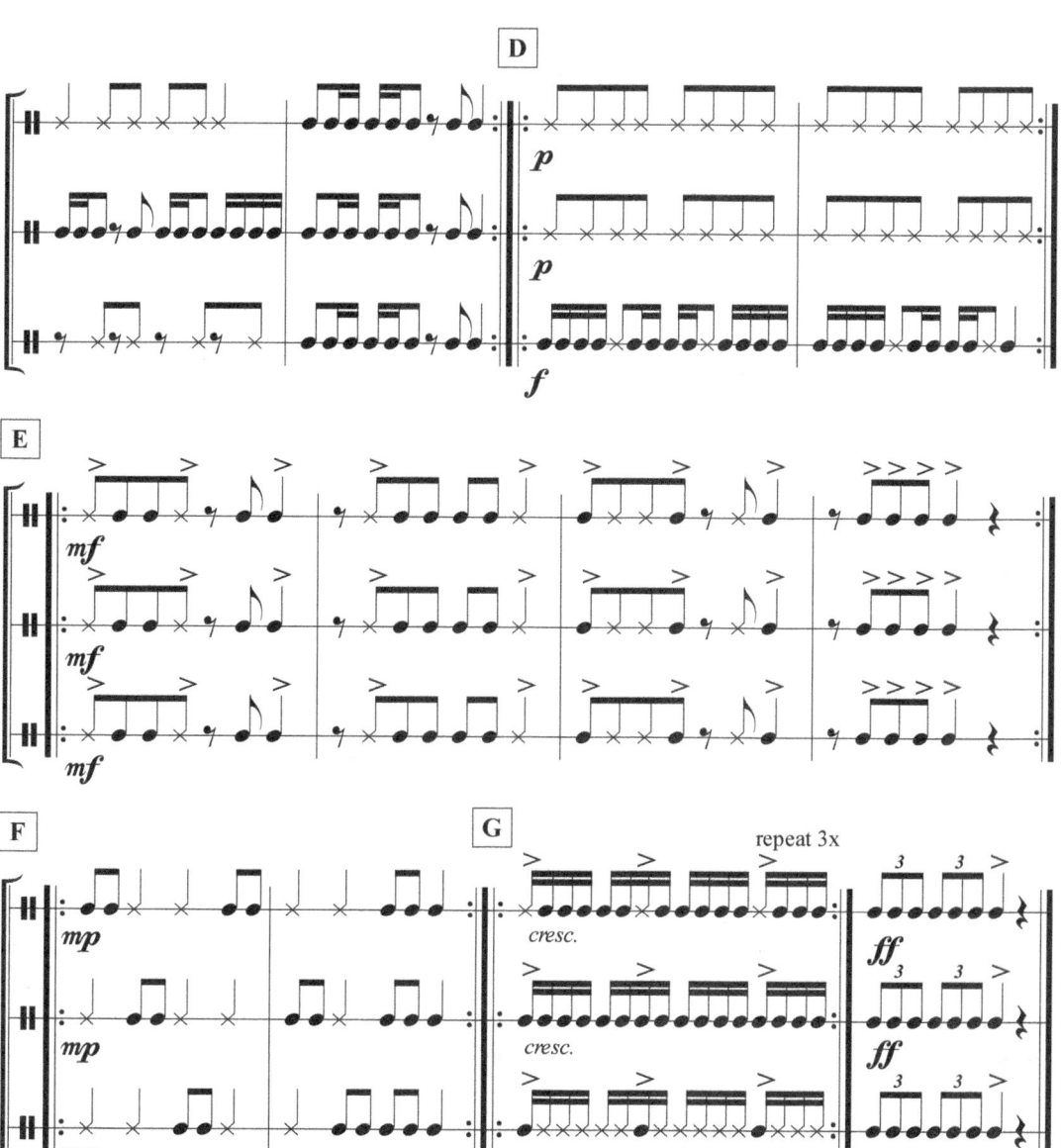

Bucket Busters

Bucket 1

mm = 125

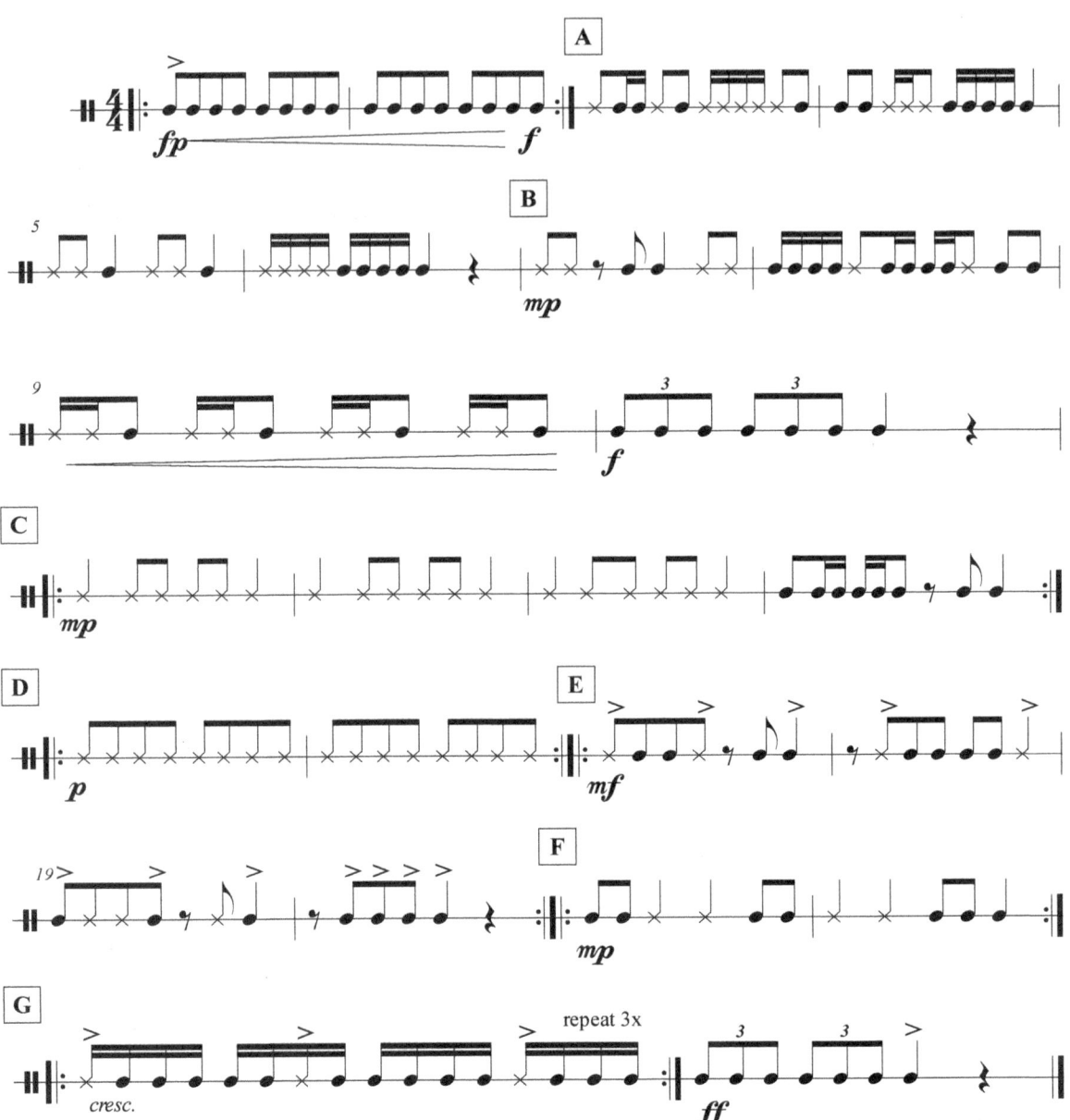

162

Rim: x

Center: standard notation

Bucket 2

mm = 125

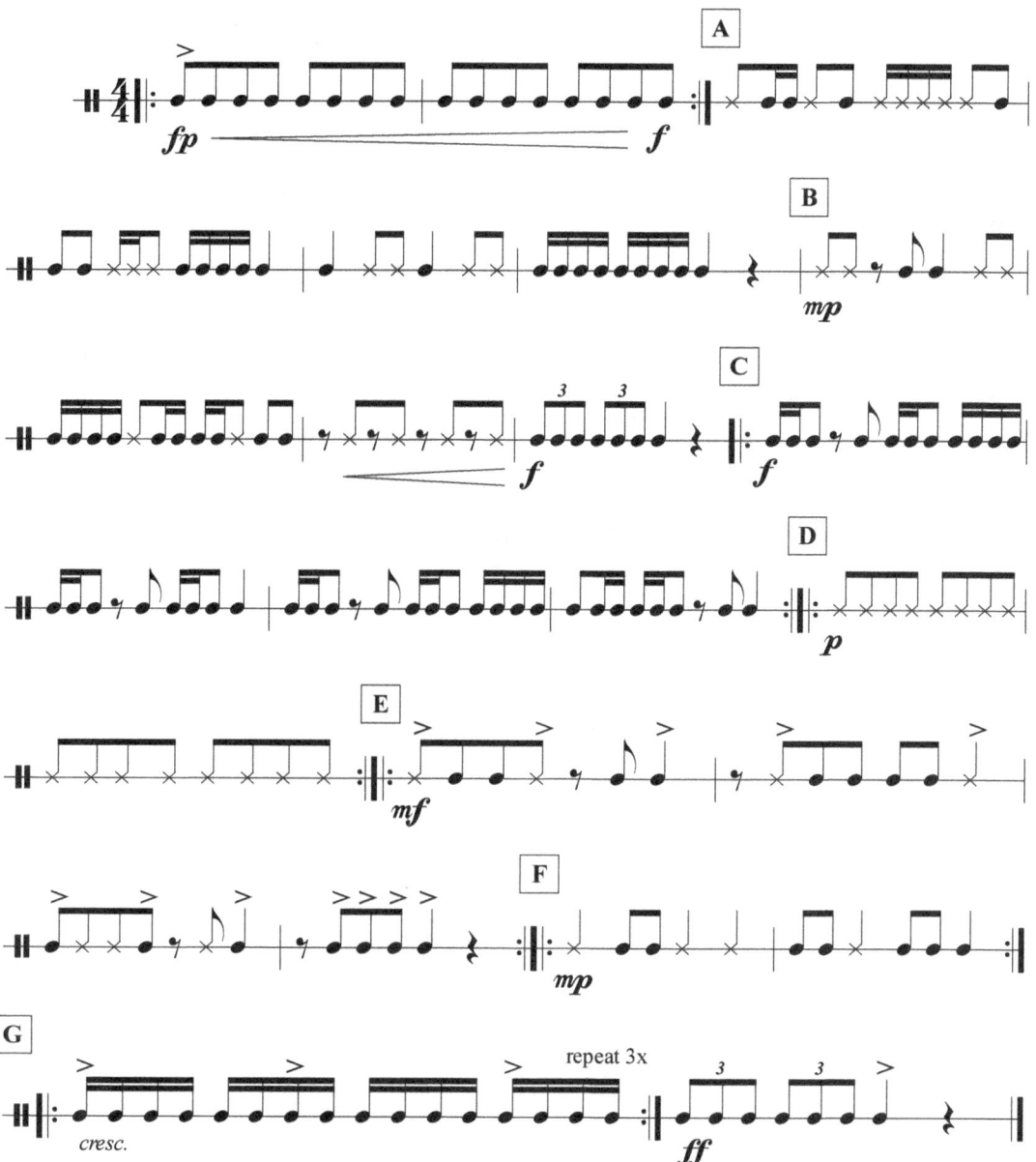

Rim: x

Center: standard notation

Bucket 3

mm = 125

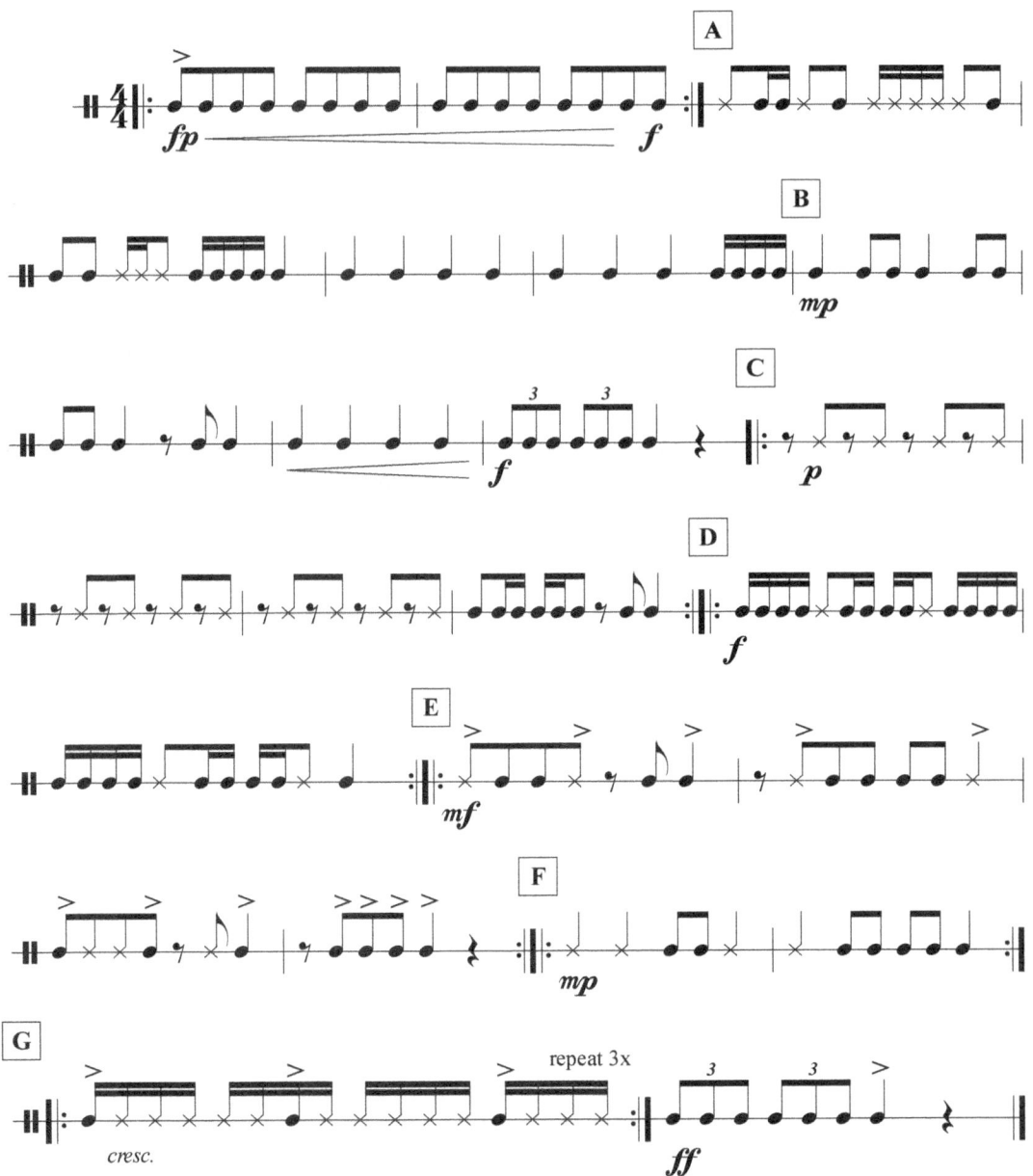

Rim: x

Center: standard notation

Pangaea

Drum Score

Enter one at a time from the bottom, and vamp until everyone is in.

Drum Score Part 1

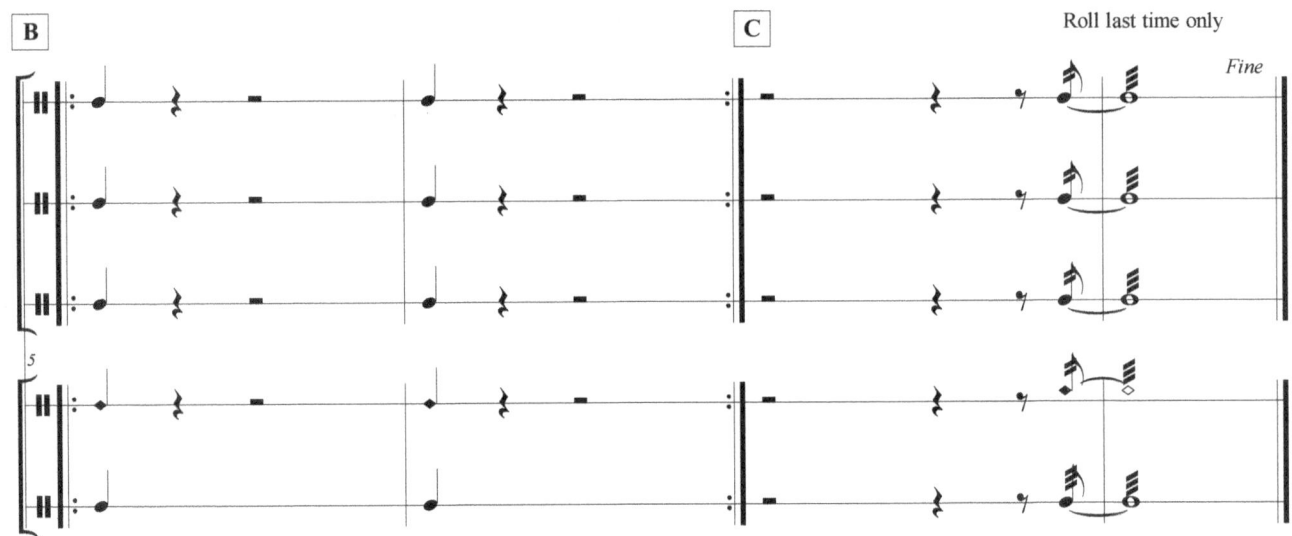

Drum Score Part 2

D Percussion Break

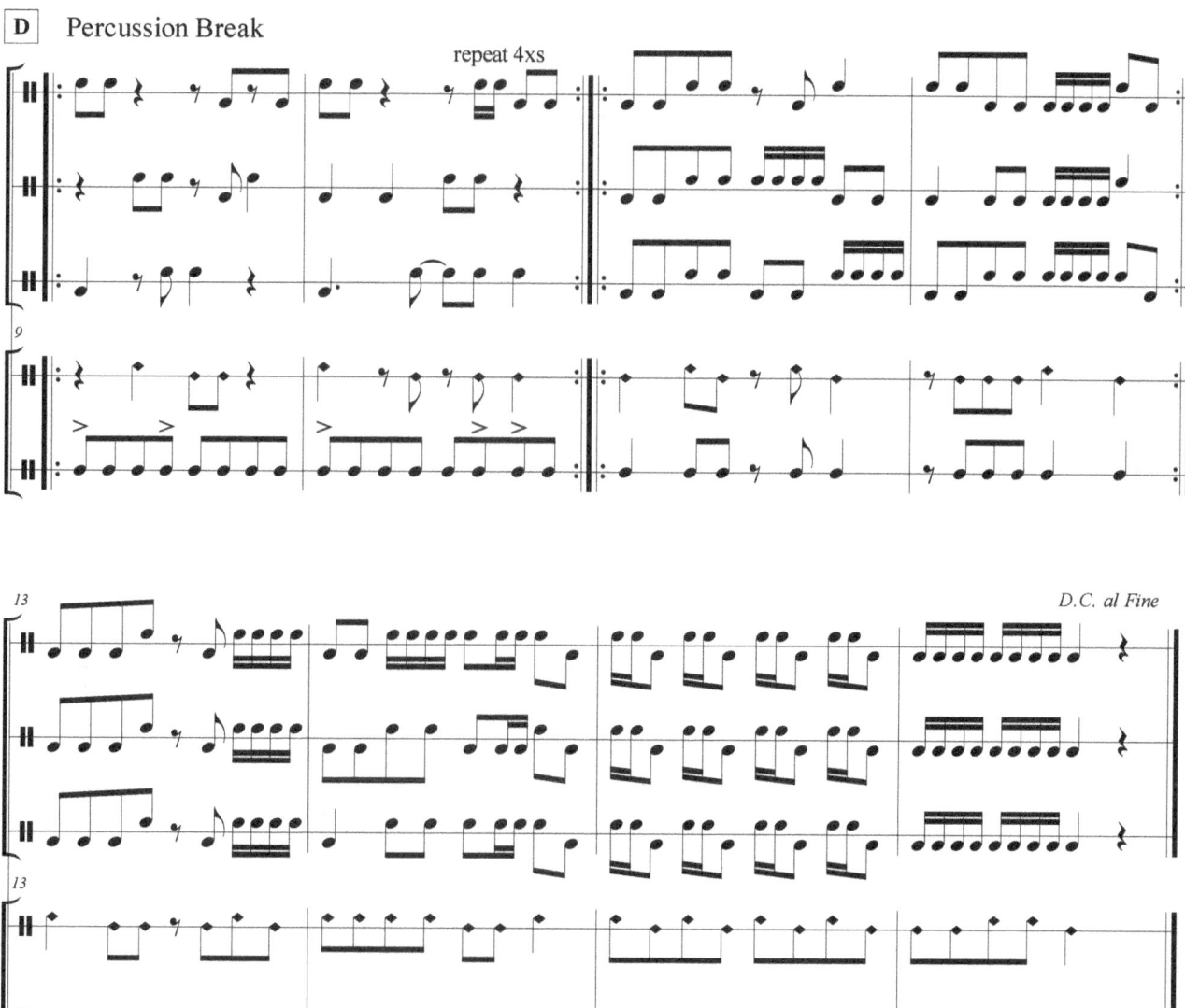

Time to empty out your percussion cabinet! Handheld percussion parts can be doubled using different instruments. During percussion break, feel free to improvise and take turns soloing.

Mallets

Enter one at a time from the bottom, and vamp until everyone is in.

How to Play Chord Changes

Chord changes are letters above a staff that tell the performer to play the root (first note of a scale), the third, and fifth. These notes can be played at the same time, arpeggiated, or in a combination of the two. Some chord changes have numbers after them. The 7 next to a letter is the most common. This means to play the seventh note of the scale down a half step. For example, when you see a C7, that means to play the C E G B♭. An *m* next to a chord change indicates that the third should be lowered by a half step, making the chord minor.

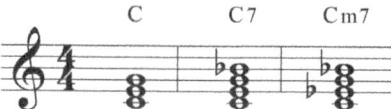

If you are playing with just two mallets, I recommend playing the third and fifth if someone else is playing the root. If no one is playing the root, then I recommend playing the root and third.

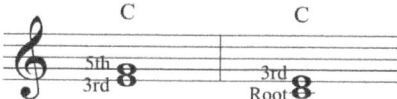

Now, if there is someone playing the roots and it's a jazz song, I recommend playing the guide tones. Guide tones are the notes that give the chord the color, and they are the third and seventh. When considering note movement (voice leading), it is common to move to the closest notes of the next chord.

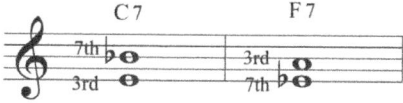

Once you know what notes to play, the next step is to decide what rhythms to play. The style of music helps to dictate this.

Example from "African Welcome Song":

Example from "Fly Me Home":

Swing

Example from "Four Seasons":

Even eighths with Alberti bass line

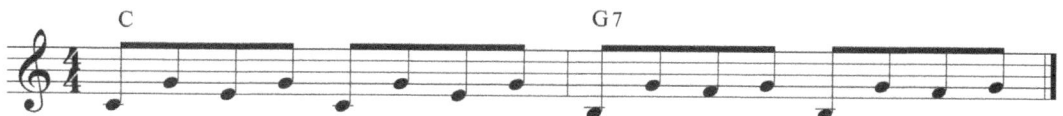

Final Thoughts

Being a percussionist in this modern era requires an accumulation of many skills on varying instruments. The intention of this book was to provide you with a strong foundation in each area of percussion. I hope that this book acts like building blocks for the development of your further percussion study and aids you in current and future ensembles you will play in. I can't stress enough the importance of having a well-rounded percussion education. The more aspects of percussion you are more familiar with, the more marketable you will be once you are ready to perform in ensembles outside the school setting. Many of the percussionists mentioned in this book began their careers while still in school. They worked hard to master their craft to rise above the rest. Once you have mastered the elements in this book, you, too, can be on your way to a successful career in music. Even if music becomes just a hobby, I hope the discipline from music study carries over into your other endeavors and the love for music stays with you forever.

Percussionists You Should Know

Classical Percussion

Anthony Cirone
Buster Bailey
Neil Grover
Morris Goldenberg
Christopher Lamb
Alan Abel

Marimba

Keiko Abe
Leigh Stevens
Gordon Stout
Nancy Zeltsman
Evelyn Glennie
Clair Omar Musser

Timpani

John Beck
Vic Firth
Saul Goodman
Fred Hinger

World Percussion

Tito Puente
Candido
Changuito
Pancho Sanchez
Giovanni Hildago
Mongo Santamaria
Valerie Naranjo
Babatunde Olatunji

Jazz Vibraphone

Lionel Hampton
Gary Burton
Red Norvo
Milt Jackson
Bobby Hutchenson
Joe Locke
Dave Samules
Stefon Harris

Drum Set: Jazz

Buddy Rich
Art Blakey
Philly Joe Jones
Max Roach
Tony Williams
Gene Krupa
Joe Morello

Drum Set: Rock

John Bonham
Neil Peart
Ringo Starr
Terry Bozzio
Jeff Picarro
Mike Portnoy

171

Glossary

Accent: Play note stronger.

Accidental: Raises or lowers the pitch of a note.

Adagio: Slow and stately.

Allegro: Fast, quickly.

Andante: Moderately slow walking tempo.

Bar Lines: Separate measures.

Chord: Three or more notes played at the same time.

Clef: Places a note on the staff.

Crescendo: Gradually get louder.

Da Capo: Directs performer to go to the top of the music.

Dal Segnio: Directs performer to go to the sign.

Decrescendo. Gradually get softer.

Dot: Adds half the note value of a note.

Double Bar Line: Shows the end of a section or end of the song.

Dynamics: The louds and softs in music.

Fermata: Directs performer to hold the note longer than its note value.

First and Second Endings: Play the first ending and go back to the repeat sign. The second time through, skip the first ending and proceed to the second ending.

Flat♭: Lowers a note by a half step.

Forte: Strong.

Harmony: Two or more notes played at the same time.

Idiophone: A percussion instrument made of metal, wood, or plastic.

Improvisation: Creation of music while you perform.

Interval: Distance between two notes.

Jazz: An American music style that came out of New Orleans in the early 1900s.

Key Signature: Indicates what flats or sharps are to be played in a song.

Largo: Broadly.

Ledger Lines: Lines above and below the staff.

Legato: Long and connecting.

Lento: Slow.

Marimba: A melodic percussion instrument with tuned bars made of wood. The bars sit on a frame with resonators (pipes) below each bar to project the sound.

Measures: Space where music is written.

Melody: A string of notes arranged together to form one idea.

Membranophone: A percussion instrument with a skin stretched across a frame.

Mezzo Forte: Medium strong.

Mezzo Piano: Medium soft.

Moderato: Moderate.

Natural ♮: Cancels the previous sharp or flat and returns the note to its original pitch.

Orchestra Bells: A percussion instrument with metal bars chromatically sequenced and struck with mallets. Also known as the glockenspiel.

Percussion: Any instrument that can be struck, shaken, or scraped.

Pianissimo: Very soft.

Piano: Soft.

Presto: Extremely fast.

Repeat Signs: Tell you to go back and play a section or measure.

Rudiments: Exercises for snare drum players to strengthen their hands.

Scale: A progression of ascending and descending notes.

Sharp ♯: Raises a note by a half step.

Snare Drum: A percussion instrument consisting of two drumheads on either side of a shell. The bottom head has a string of vibrating metal strands that run from one side to the other.

Staccato: Play the note shorter; half the note value.

Staff: The five lines on which music is written.

Time Signature: Top number: Number of beats in a measure; bottom number: Tells what note gets what beat.

Timpani: A tuned percussion instrument made usually of a copper bowl with a tunable head on top. The tuning is controlled by the foot and sometimes the hand.

Traps: Handheld percussion instruments.

Vibraphone: A metal-plated tuned percussion instrument with a frame and resonators (pipes) below each bar to project the sound. Inside the pipes are oscillating fans that give a waver to the pitch. The notes are sustained with a foot pedal.

Vivace: Lively and fast.

Xylophone: A hard wooden-barred melodic percussion instrument that sits on a frame with resonators (pipes) below each bar to project the sound.

Bibliography

Berheide, B., et al. (1990). *Percussion education: A source book of concepts and information.* Indianapolis, IN: Percussive Arts Society.

Bradley, J. (2002, April–May). The short music lesson: Success in half an hour a week. *The American Music Teacher,* 51, 20–31.

Buyer, P. (2002, April–May). Inside the private lesson. *The American Music Teacher, 51,* 15–19.

Crawford, Stephen. (2005). Building a better percussion section. Retrieved from Jupiter Band Instruments, Inc., website: http://www.jupitermusic.com/buildingpercuss.html.

De Almeida, H. (2005) *Brazilian rhythms for the drum set.* New York: Carl Fisher, LLC.

Firth, V., & Feldstein, S. (2001). *Snare drum, a comprehensive musical method for individual or group instruction and performance.* Boston: PalyinTime.

Grifa, R. (1995, March). Beyond just drumming: Teaching percussionists to be musicians. *The Instrumentalist, 50,* 5–9.

Grover, N., & Whaley, G. (1997). *The art of tambourine and triangle playing* (Meredith Music Publications). Milwaukee, WI: Hal Leonard Corporation.

Holloway, R., & Bartlett, H. (1964). *Guide to teaching percussion* (4th ed.). Dubuque, IA: Wm. C. Brown.

Isaak, C. (2006). *African rhythms and beats.* Burlington, VT: JPMC Music.

Mixon, K. (2004, July). More efficient rehearsals. *The Instrumentalist, 58,* 12, 38–40.

Mueller, K. (1972). *Teaching total percussion.* West Nyack, NY: Parker.

National Association for Music Education. (2005). Pull-out music instruction. Retrieved from the NAfME website: http://www.menc.org/connect/surveys/position/pulloutdraft.html

National Middle School Association. (1995). *This we believe.* Columbus, OH: Author.

Peters, G. (1995, August). The amazing growth of percussion ensembles. *The Instrumentalist, 50*(1), 176–183.

Popejoy, J. (2005, October). Don't forget your percussionists! Tips for getting the most out of your percussion section. *Tempo, 60*(1), 66.

Rendon, V. (2001). *The art of playing timbales* (Vol. 1). Columbus, OH: Music in Motion Ltd.

Sanchez, P. (2002). *Conga cookbook.* New York: Cherry Lane Music Co.

Schmid W. (1998). *World music drumming, across cultural curriculum.* Milwaukee, WI: Hal Leonard Corporation.

Stewart, S. (2005, August). Tips on teaching middle school, an interview with Charles Jackson. *The Instrumentalist, 60*(1), 20.

Walker, D. (1998). *Teaching music, managing the successful music program* (2nd ed.). New York: Schirmer Books.

Whaley, G. (2004, July). Solving rhythm problems. *The Instrumentalist, 58*(12), 16. http://en.wikipedia.org/wiki/Tempo

http://en.wikipedia.org/wiki/Giovanni_Hidalgo

http://en.wikipedia.org/wiki/Lionel_Hampton

http://en.wikipedia.org/wiki/Gary_Burton

http://en.wikipedia.org/wiki/Keiko_Abe

http://www.anthonyjcirone.com/Resume_ep_41-1.html

Bibliography

http://en.wikipedia.org/wiki/Buddy_Rich

http://www.pas.org/experience/halloffame/BaileyBuster.aspx

http://en.wikipedia.org/wiki/Leigh_Howard_Stevens

http://www.pas.org/About/the-society/experience/halloffame/GoodmanSaul.aspx

http://en.wikipedia.org/wiki/Vic_Firth

http://en.wikipedia.org/wiki/Babatunde_Olatunji

http://www.pas.org/experience/halloffame/AbelAlan.aspx

http://en.wikipedia.org/wiki/Neil_Peart

Acknowledgments

So many people supported me and encouraged me to develop this method of percussion study, and I would like to take the opportunity to thank them. God, for giving me the clarity to develop this system of study. My family: Tricia, Adam, and Sarah Colaneri; Paul DiFrancesco; and Mom and Dad, of course. Norman Hirschy from Oxford University Press, John Fitzgerald and Mike DeMenno from Remo. Rob Wilson Photography, Joe Lanni. The great percussion educators in New Jersey: Leigh Stevens from Malletech, Gary Mallinson, Yale Snyder, Andy Veiss, Nora Morrison, Sharon Silverstein, Alex Bocchino, Dean Witten and Dr. Rick Dammers from Rowan University, Dr. Maridea Warren and Dr. Stellio Dubbiosi from New Jersey City University, Daryl Bott from Masson Gross School of the Arts. Models Renee Cabato, Charlie Margulies, Brennan Hector, Kelly Hector, Patrick Keller, Chris Keller, John Santucci, Jason Wiedman, and the great students and administration in the Berkeley Heights Public School System.

About the Author

Since 1996, Chris Colaneri has been directing percussion ensembles and steel pan ensembles, leading drum circles, and giving group percussion lessons in the New York and New Jersey public schools systems. He recently cofounded and is currently the president of the New Jersey Percussion Educators Association.

As a vibist, marimbist, and Latin percussion performer, Chris has led his own jazz quartet, CCQ, since 1997. This ensemble has given featured performances at the New Jersey Performing Art Center, various jazz clubs, private corporate and political functions, and jazz festivals throughout New Jersey. His orchestral endeavors have taken him to Spain, France, Israel, and Jordan, where he has given many radio and television appearances. As a freelance percussionist for more than 25 years, Chris has performed with steel pan groups, African dance ensembles, brass ensembles, local orchestras, wedding bands, and community musical theater companies. Currently, he is in preparation for his next project as a solo multimedia multipercussionist. Chris's recordings span genres including the styles of jazz, classical, meditation, hip-hop, and rock.

In an endeavor to promote total percussion in public schools systems, Chris has written articles for the New Jersey music educators' magazine, *Tempo*, and his recent book, *Incorporating Total Percussion into the Middle School Band Program*, has been published through VDM Publishing House. Chris has given percussion clinics at many public schools and Days of Percussions throughout New Jersey, and he has presented at the New Jersey Music Educators' state convention. He has also given workshops at Rowan University and Mason Gross School of the Arts on aspects of developing a total percussion philosophy.

Chris also arranges and composes for percussion ensembles and steel pan ensembles. His solo marimba arrangement of "Take 5" has been published through MalletWorks. With all his experience as a music educator and performer, it was a natural progression for Chris to develop the Pulse Percussion Ensemble, a student-based intergenerational ensemble that gives public performances at local minor league ball parks, country fairs, and malls. During the holidays, this group of more than 50 percussionists from all over New Jersey turns into Holiday Percussion and plays rockin' holiday music. For more about Chris and his ensembles, you can visit his personal website at www.ccmallets.com.

Index